BIBLE KEY WORDS

XIII. WRATH

BIBLE KEY WORDS
FROM GERHARD KITTEL'S
*THEOLOGISCHES WÖRTERBUCH
ZUM NEUEN TESTAMENT*

WRATH

BY

H. KLEINKNECHT, J. FICHTNER,
G. STÄHLIN ET AL.

ADAM & CHARLES BLACK
LONDON

FIRST PUBLISHED 1964
A. AND C. BLACK LIMITED
4, 5 AND 6 SOHO SQUARE, LONDON W.1

Translated from the German
by Dorothea M. Barton, M.A.
edited by P. R. Ackroyd, PH.D.
© 1964 A. & C. Black Ltd.

PRINTED IN GREAT BRITAIN AT
THE ABERDEEN UNIVERSITY PRESS

EDITOR'S PREFACE

THIS book is a translation of the article ὀργή in the *Theologisches Wörterbuch sum Neuen Testament* (TWNT), begun by G. Kittel and now edited by G. Friedrich, Vol. V, pp. 382-448. The writing of this article was originally undertaken by O. Procksch. After his death in 1947, H. Kleinknecht, O. Grether, E. Sjöberg, and G. Stählin shared the work between them. When Grether died suddenly in the summer of 1949, J. Fichtner completed the Old Testament part. The statements to which the name of O. Procksch is attached are derived from his manuscript, part of which was placed at the disposal of the authors. Apart from some fairly substantial abbreviation in Chapter I and some curtailing of footnotes, the whole text is here translated and the order follows exactly that of the German original.

Although this particular article stands under the heading of ὀργή, its authors have in fact recognised that there is a wide range of terms used in both Hebrew and Greek to cover the ideas of wrath and anger for which English also has a variety of terms, and it has been clearly recognised that no one term covers the idea of wrath whether in the Old Testament or the New. That this is termed a Bible Word Book is appropriate enough, but it differs from some others in this series in that it is primarily a study of the problem of understanding the divine nature when it is described in terms of wrath, a description which we may recognise as real even while acknowledging the inadequacy of our terms. This inadequacy of terminology has long been recognised and in Chapters III and IV in particular, attention is drawn to early paraphrases designed to avoid what was felt to be excessive anthropopathism. But the difficulty of terminology and our consciousness that whatever terms we use for the nature of God are inevitably conditioned by the background to our own thinking, does not absolve us from the need to clarify our minds in thinking about the nature of a God whose love may be appropriately described as a burning fire (Deut. iv.24) and with whom is forgiveness that He may be feared (Ps. cxxx.4).

All Hebrew words have been transliterated and, where necessary, translated. Greek words are not transliterated. Where quotations are given from elsewhere than the New Testament (or Septuagint), a translation has been given, except where the meaning is evident or where the actual Greek word used is of particular importance. In a number of cases translations have been given of crucial Greek and Latin words, but these are to be taken only as rough guides to the meaning, since, as will appear from their contents, these are words which are deserving of full and separate study. Such of them as appear in the New Testament are, of course, so treated in other volumes of TWNT.

Biblical references follow the normal chapter and verse enumeration of the Hebrew and Greek texts, with a note of deviations in the English versions. References to the Septuagint therefore in some cases require modification, particularly in the Psalter and in the book of Jeremiah.

CONTENTS

BIBLIOGRAPHY

GENERAL

H. CREMER: *Biblisch-theologisches Wörterbuch des neutestamentlichen Griechisch*, ed. J. Kögel ([11]1923).

LIDDELL and SCOTT: *Greek-English Lexicon* ([7]1940).

W. PAPE: *Griechisch-Deutsches Handwörterbuch*, ed. M. Sengebusch ([3]1880).

F. PASSOW: *Wörterbuch der griechischen Sprache* ([5]1841 ff.): new ed. W. Crönert (1913 ff.).

E. PREUSCHEN: *Griechisch-deutsches Wörterbuch . . . NT*, ed. W. Bauer ([5]1958). ET of edn. 4 (1949 ff.) by W. F. Arndt and F. W. Gingrich (1957), sv (Pr.-Bauer).

J. H. H. SCHMIDT: *Synonymik der griechischen Sprache*, III (1879), pp. 551-572.

R. C. TRENCH, *Synonyms of the New Testament* ([15]1906), pp. 123-127 (§37 θυμός, ὀργή, παροργισμός).

A. RUEGG: 'Zorn Gottes', in RE[3] 21, 719-729.

A. BERTHOLET, H. GUNKEL, W. MUNDLE: 'Zorn Gottes', in RGG, V ([2]1931), 2133-2136.

A. RITSCHL: *De Ira Dei* (1859).

—— *Die christliche Lehre von der Rechtfertigung und der Versöhnung*, II ([3]1889), pp. 119-156.

R. BARTOLOMÄI: 'Vom Zorn Gottes', in Jahrbücher für deutsche Theologie 6 (1891), pp. 256-277.

F. WEBER: *Vom Zorne Gottes* (1862).

A. DIECKMANN: 'Die christliche Lehre vom Zorne Gottes', ZwTh NF 1, II (1893), pp. 321-377.

R. OTTO: *Das Heilige* ([26-28], 1947), pp. 18-20, 91f., 101, 116-118, ET, *The Idea of the Holy* (rev. edn. 1928), cf. Index, 'Wrath of God'.

—— *Gottheit und Gottheiten der Arier* (1932), pp. 50-64.

ORIGEN: *Contra Celsum*, IV, 71-73 (GCS, Orig. I, 340-343). Cf. H. Chadwick, *Contra Celsum* (1953)

LACTANTIUS: *De Ira dei* (CSEL, 27, I, 65-132), and on this cf. W. KUTSCH, *In Lactanti de ira dei librum quaestiones philologae* = Klassisch-philologische Studien, 6 (1933).

M. POHLENZ: *Vom Zorne Gottes* = FRL 12 (1909).

Chapter I

Aristotle: *Rhetoric*, II, 2, p. 1378, a, 31-1380, a, 4.

Stobaeus: *Eclogues*, III, 20 (Wachsmuth-Hense, III, pp. 539-566).

Philodemus Philosophus: *De Ira* (ed. Wilke, 1914).

Plutarch: *De Ira Cohibenda* (II, 452e-464d).

Seneca: *De Ira*.

J. Irmscher: *Götterzorn bei Homer* (1950).

W. Marg: *Der Charakter in der Sprache der frühgriechischen Dichtung*, Kieler Arbeiten zur klassischen Philologie I (1938), pp. 13 f.

R. Camerer; *Zorn und Groll in der sophokleischer Tragödie*. Diss. Freiburg (1930) especially pp. 52-64.

K. Latte: 'Schuld und Sünde in der griechischen Religion', ARW 20 (1920-21) pp. 257-260.

R. Hirzel: *Themis, Dike und verwandtes* (1907), pp. 138, 416-418.

Chapter II

C. von Orelli: 'Einige alttestamentliche Prämisse zur neutesta-mentlichen Versöhnungslehre', ZWL, 5 (1884), pp. 22-33.

J. Böhmer: 'Zorn', ZAW, 44 (1926), pp. 320-322.

P. Volz: *Das Dämonische in Jahwe* (1924).

Cf. also, the discussions of the theology of the Old Testament, especially E. König: (^{34}1923), pp. 173-177; W. Eichrodt, I (^{3}1948), pp. 124-131; ET of edn. 6 (1959), (1960), pp. 258-269; E. Sellin: (1936) *passim*.

Chapter IV

Weber (cf. above): pp. 155, 161, 172, 314.

W. Bousset and H. Gressmann = W. Bousset, *Die Religion des Judentums im späthellenistischen Zeitalter*, ed. W. Gressmann (^{3}1926), pp. 350 f.

H. L. Strack and P. Billerbeck: *Kommentar zum NT aus Talmud und Midrasch*, I-V (^{2}1956), see III, pp. 30 f. (Str. B.).

E. Sjöberg: *Gott und die Sünder im palästinischen Judentum*, = BWANT, F, 4, H, 27 (1939), Index sv 'Zorn Gottes'.

Chapter V, 1

Strack and Billerbeck (see above): I, pp. 276-278; III, p. 645.

M. Dibelius: *Jakobusbrief* (^{7}1921), pp. 104-106.

F. Hauck: *Jakobusbrief* (1926) pp. 74 f., n. 30.

Th. Rüther: *Die sittliche Förderung der Apatheia in den beiden ersten christlichen Jahrhunderten und bei Clement von Alexandrien* = Freiburger Theologische Studien, 23 (1949).

CHAPTER V, 2

E. VON DOBSCHÜTZ: *Theologie*, p. 79.

A. SCHLATTER: *Römerbrief*, pp. 46-54.

G. P. WETTER: *Der Vergeltungsgedanke bei Paulus* (1912), pp. 16–55.

F. V. FILSON: *St. Paul's conception of Recompense* (1931), pp. 39-48.

H. BRAUN: *Gerichtsgedanke und Rechtvertigungslehre bei Paulus* (1930), especially pp. 41-44.

G. BORNKAMM: 'Die Offenbarung des Zornes Gottes (Röm i-iii), ZNW 34 (1935), pp. 239-262.

G. SCHRENK: *Unser Glaube an den Zorn Gottes nach dem Römerbrief* (1944).

A. VON JÜCHEN: *Der Zorn Gottes* (1948).

Cf. also the discussions in the theologies of the New Testament, especially in H. J. HOLTZMANN, II ([2]1911), pp. 57 f. H. WEINEL ([8]1928), pp. 109, 260 f., 322 f. P. FEINE ([7]1936), pp. 206-208. R. BULTMANN (1948), pp. 76, 283 f., ETI (1952), pp. 75 f., 288.

Reference to works mentioned in this bibliography is normally by the name of the author alone.

ABBREVIATIONS

ANET	Ancient Near Eastern Texts, ed. Pritchard (1950).
AOT	*Altorientalische Texte zum AT* (²1926).
ARW	Archiv für Religionswissenschaft (1898 ff.).
ASG	Abhandlungen der Kgl. Sächsischen Gesellschaft der Wissenschaften (phil. hist. Klasse).
BH³	Biblia Hebraica (³Kittel).
BWANT	Beiträge zur Wissenschaft vom Alten und Neuen Testament.
CAF	*Comicorum Atticorum Fragmenta*, ed. Th. Koch. (1880 ff.).
CD	Cairo Damascus Covenant (= Zadokite Document).
Cr.-Kö.	H. Cremer: *Biblisch-theologisches Wörterbuch des ntlichen Griechisch*, ed. J. Kögel (¹¹1923).
CSEL	*Corpus Scriptorum Ecclesiasticorum Latinorum* (1866 ff.)
Ditt Syll	W. Dittenberger, *Sylloge Inscriptionum Graecarum*, I-IV, 1, 2 (³1915-24).
DOTT	Documents from OT Times, ed. Winton Thomas (1958).
BZAW	Beihefte der Zeitschrift für die alttestamentliche Wissenschaft.
ET	English translation.
EVV	English versions.
FRL	Forschungen zur Religion und Literatur des AT und NT.
GCS	*Die griechischen christlichen Schriftsteller* (1899 ff.).
JSS	Journal of Semitic Studies.
MT	Masoretic text.
NEB	New English Bible.
NTD	Das Neue Testament Deutsch.
Pr-Bauer	cf. Bibliography.
RE³	*Realencyclopaedie für protestantische Theologie und Kirche* (³1896 ff.).
RGG	*Religion in Geschichte und Gegenwart* (²1927 ff.).
Stob. Ecl.	Stobaeus *Eclogae*.
Str. B.	Strack-Billerbeck, cf. Bibliography.
sv	*sub voce*.
TGF	*Tragicorum Graecorum Fragmenta*, ed. A. Nauck (²1899).
TWNT	*Theologisches Wörterbuch zum Neuen Testament*, ed. G. Friedrich.
ZAW	Zeitschrift für die alttestamentliche Wissenschaft.
ZNW	Zeitschrift für die neutestamentliche Wissenschaft.
ZSTh.	Zeitschrift für systematische Theologic.
ZWL	Zeitschrift für kirchliche Wissenschaft und Kirchliches Leben.
ZwTh.	Zeitschrift für wissenschaftliche Theologic.

I. WRATH IN CLASSICAL ANTIQUITY

1. *The meaning of the word ὀργή*

ὀργή is a post-Homeric word, attested for the first time in Hesiod, *Opera* 304. From then onwards it is frequent in poetry and prose. Corresponding to its affinity with ὀργάω/ὀργάς which means the *luxuriant rising of sap and energy*, the *impelling and germinating activity in nature*, it was originally in general (*a*) the *impulsive behaviour* of man and beast, especially the *impulsive state of the human spirit* which breaks out actively in external behaviour in contrast to the more internal and quiet ἦθος (cf. Plat. *Leg.* X.908e). When ὀργή is asserted of men's character and nature, comparisons with animals and the like point expressly to the natural aspect of the concept (cf. Hesiod, *Op.* 303). In the general sense of individual character and nature ὀργή becomes important particularly in Attic tragedy and a factor in the tragic happenings. In the ὀργή the insight or judgement of a man—whether it be true or false—takes shape and drives him to the decisive act.

As contrasted with this earlier usage the content of the meaning of ὀργή became, already in tragedy, more specialised and restricted: soon ὀργή denotes only a quite definite reaction of the human soul, i.e. (*b*) *wrath* as being the manifestation, with the most violent external effect, of the vehement internal protest of the θυμός.[1] Whilst on the one hand both concepts stand side by side and complete each other, yet on the other hand ὀργή differs from θυμός because it has the characteristic of being directed to an object, namely vengeance or punishment with a significant intention. ὀργή which already in tragedy always seeks to preserve something

[1] cf. TWNT III, pp. 167 f.

that is recognised to be right, became then in the national life of later times the characteristic and legitimate attitude of the judge who has to avenge the wrong. In consequence there appears as a regular formula in legal language δεινὸν καὶ ὀργῆς ἄξιον (*a monstrous and scandalous offence* lit. *deserving of wrath*) in Demosth. *Or.* 9.31; 19.7, etc. Here ὀργή is not intended to refer to the verdict (Aristot. *Rhet.* I.1, p. 1354a, 16 ff.) but only to the assessment of the punishment.[1] This conception led to ὀργή gradually itself assuming the meaning (*c*) *punishment* (cf. Demosth. *Or.* 21.147; Lycurgus, *Contra Leocratem* 138).

Apart from the moral anger which restrains the wicked[2] and is sometimes described explicitly as δικάια ὀργή (Demosth. *Or.* 16.19; Dio Cassius, 40.51.2; Ditt. Syll. 780.22), ὀργή came to be used in Greek principally in a negative sense.[3] As *irritability* it is already associated in tragedy with blind[4] purposes and fancies by which man allows himself to be driven; it appears as the regular antithesis to γνώμη (Soph. *Oed. Tyr.* 523 f.), λόγος and λογισμός (Menander fr. 630 [CAF IV.188]; Thuc. II.11, 4 f.; Aristot. fr. 661 [ed. by Rose]), to the σοφόν (Eur. fr. 760 [TGF 397]). It is not only itself a useless evil (Eur. *Med.* 446 f.), but is necessarily accompanied by many other evils (Chairemon fr. 28 [TGF]). Therefore the ethical claim of philosophy demands that man should be the master of this emotional disturbance which does not even stop short before the gods. Whilst Academics and Peripatetics explain anger as natural, indeed as necessary for great deeds and virtues, above all for warlike bravery, and only aim at moderating and guiding anger by reason, in the opinion of the Stoics

---

[1] cf. Hirzel, pp. 416-418; Pohlenz, p. 15, n. 3.
[2] cf. Theophr. in Sen. *De Ira* I.14: *non potest fieri, ut non vir bonus irascitur malis.*   [3] cf. the plentiful examples in Stob. *Ecl.*
[4] cf. Chrysipp. fr. 390 (von Arnim III.94, 43 ff.).

ὀργή and its like is one of the chief passions to be stamped out as far as possible.[1] This ethical idea was then asserted by philosophy in a special manner with regard to the anger of the deity.

2. *The wrath of the gods amongst the Greeks*

Angry gods dwell so powerfully in the consciousness of mankind that some have wished to explain all worship as being the attempt to forestall the anger of the gods or to appease it. This is an accepted fact already in pre-Homeric religion.[2] Pre-Greek divinities of the earth and divinities which bring curses, like the Erinys, have anger as their nature even in their names 'the Furies'. Instinctive, merciless and terrible as nature itself, they appear in every place where its inviolable bonds—primarily of blood and the family, but then later also of the law—are being broken and demand retaliation. Then since Homer the anger of the gods in Greek mythology and poetry is 'a mighty and effective force in the interplay of the forces amongst the powers controlling fate',[3] i.e. of reality struggling to prevail. It appears in a twofold form, occurring firstly amongst the gods themselves and secondly directed against men. In both cases it is a form of self-assertion and of protest, whether it be the conflict of particular divine claims to exist which contradict each other (Hom. *Il.*8.407, 421) or the reaction against men's overstepping their bounds, as for instance presumption towards the gods (*Il.* 24. 606), neglect of sacrifices (*Il.* 5.177 f.; 9.533-538), failure to respect priests (*Il.*1.44, 75), to observe the rights of hospitality (*Od.* 2.66 f.; 14.283), to honour the dead (*Il.* 22.358; *Od.* 11.73), etc. All this provokes divine anger which is difficult to propitiate, which leads to no

[1] *Stoici . . . voluerant eam* (sc. *iram*) *penitus excidere.* Chrysipp. fr. 444 (von Arnim III.108.34 ff.).

[2] cf. U. von Wilamovitz, *Der Glaube der Hellenen* I (1931), p. 35.

[3] W. Schadewaldt, *Iliasstudien* (1938), p. 154, n. 1.

good (*Od.* 3.135, 145), and before which it is better to retreat (*Il.* 5.443 f.). Here anger and wrath are not so much anthropomorphic traits of character but rather something to which the god has a kind of right because his claim to existence has been slighted. In so far as this means that the restoration of an appointed state is demanded, and independent existence is helped to assert itself or a decree of fate is carried out, the anger of the gods is not blind in its rage but clear-sighted and, in regard to men, is in a negative manner the honour which they do to him by indicating his nature or by confining him within the limits assigned to him in order that in them he may be what he is.

All this is not expressed at first by ὀργή which in any case is not a Homeric word, but by χόλος[1] and κότος (*anger*)[2] and especially by the term μῆνις (*anger*)[3] with its related words derived from the sacral sphere and almost exclusively confined to it.[4] It is first in tragedy that ὀργή appears as well to denote the anger of the gods[5] and from Euripides onwards it is used more frequently with this meaning (cf. Adespota fr. 296 [TGF 896]).[6] Whilst in Hesiod (*Op.* 47, 53) Zeus in his anger against Prometheus lets the punishment follow hard on

[1] Hom. *Il.* 15.122. Cf. Apollonius Rhodius III.337.

[2] Hom. *Od.* 11.101 ff. Cf. Aesch. *Ag.* 1211.

[3] Hom. *Il.* 5.177 f. *Il.* 21.523 describes a city which is allowed to go up in smoke and flames; *a burning city . . . lit by the wrath* (μῆνις) *of the gods*. Thus the anger of the gods can strike not only an individual, but also a city and a whole nation.

[4] The etymology and the different meanings of the numerous Homeric words for the anger of the gods are now well presented in Irmscher, pp. 3-26; cf. *ib.*, pp. 29-36 for the different ways in which Homer describes the anger of the gods.

[5] cf. the ὀργαί of the Erinys in Aesch. *Eum.* 847, 939.

[6] Here in characteristic Greek fashion we see at the same time the effects of the god's anger which starts with the νοῦς of men: *eadem ira deorum hanc eius satellibus iniecit amentiam* (Cic. *Mil.* 86). Cf. also Eur. *Iph. Taur.* 987; *Med.* 129 f.; *Hipp.* 438; 1417 f.

the heels of the offence, Solon already considers it a sign of power and greatness in the god that he does not punish at once. There is a distinction between human and divine anger (cf. Solon fr. 1.25 f. [Diehl]).[1] With reference to ὀργαί (which here no doubt keeps still to the wider meaning of (a) (cf. p. 1), Euripides says in *Ba.* 1348: it is not 'fitting' that gods should resemble mortals. The ethical and rational idea of 'what befits a god' discovered by Xenophanes is aimed in particular at the stories told by the poets (cf. e.g. Plut. *Pericl.* 39 [I.173d-e]).[2] The criticism of myth arises especially out of the philosophic requirement that the divine in accordance with its true nature should be free from every passion (Sextus Empiricus, *Pyrrh. Hyp.* I.162). Therefore Cicero can declare freedom from anger in particular to be the common property of the concept of god in all schools of philosophy (*Off.* III.102).

Epicurus begins the first sentence of the *Philosophical Maxims* with the assertion (fr. 139): *the happy and the incorruptible . . . is affected neither by wrath nor by favour: for all such things belong to weakness.*[3] We can read of the same antithesis between ὀργή and χάρις (cf. Demosth. *Or.* 19.92) in Plut. *Suav. Viv. Epic.* 22 (II.1102e). Thus the Stoic, although he too rejects ὀργή, differs from Epicurus in holding fast to the ideas of grace and succour, the good will of the deity (Letter of Aristeas, 254).[4]

---

[1] A Christian version of the idea is found in Lact. 20 f.

[2] cf. Cic. *Nat. Deor.* I.16(42): *qui* (sc. Poetae) *et ira inflammatus . . . induxerunt deos*; II.28(70): *et perturbatis animis inducuntur* (sc. dei); *accepimus enim deorum . . . iracundies—ut fabulae creduntur stultissime et plena sunt futilitatis summaeque levitatis.*

[3] On its continuing influence, cf. Lucretius, *De Rerum Natura* II.651; Philodemus Philosophus, *De Ira* col. 43 (ed. by Wilke, pp. 85-87); Posidonius in Cic. *Nat Deor.* I.44(124); I.17(45); Epic. fr. 363.365 f. (ed. by H. Usener, pp. 242-244).

[4] cf. Lact. 5.1: *existimantur Stoici . . . aliquanto melius de divinitate sensisse, qui aiunt gratiam in deo esse, iram non esse.* Lact. himself holds

In this matter the philosophical doctrines must not lead us astray; on the contrary it is just these which themselves indicate how widespread not only in poetry, but also in popular belief must have been the conception of the gods, whose anger claims propitiation and expresses itself in judgements. Plato speaks of unusually serious illnesses and sufferings which befell this or that family as a result of an old resentment of the gods for some reason or other and which were cured through the religious ecstasy of the appointed priests who have recourse to prayers and vows, acts of worship, expiatory rites and solemn functions.[1] Otherwise Lucretius would neither have striven so passionately for deliverance from the fear connected with it (cf. *De Rerum Natura* V.119 ff.; VI.71 f.; Cic. *Nat. Deor.* 17.45), nor would Plutarch have heeded to discuss the sceptics' question: *But for what reason should the wrath of the gods at first sink out of sight, like certain rivers, only to resurge later against others, leading in the end to the direst calamities? (Ser. Num. Pun.* 12 [II.557e]). For even when God punishes he does not do so from anger (Plut. *Ser. Num. Pun.* 20 [II.562d]). Plutarch is aiming chiefly at popular mythological tradition, but also at cultic representations, in which notwithstanding philosophical criticism

the view that anger and mercy are both necessary for the punishment of the wicked and the recompense of the good, if the reality of God and all religion is not to be destroyed. Just as the Christian Apologists (Aristid. *Apol.* i.6; Athenag. Suppl. 21) made use of philosophical ideas when criticising the pagan conceptions of God and mythology (cf. J. Geffcken, *Zwei griechische Apologeten* (1907), p. 40), so by contrast ancient philosophy for its part reproached the Christians with what they said concerning the ὀργὴ θεοῦ. Cf. Orig. *Cels.* IV.73. For the refutation undertaken by Origen who in the abstract supports the same ideal of the ἀπαθεία of God (VI.65), cf. Pohlenz, pp. 31-36.

[1] *Phaedr.* 244 d-e. Also F. Pfister, 'Der Wahnsinn des Weihepriesters' in *Festschrift Cimbria* (1926), pp. 55-62.

ὀργή and ὀργίζεσθαι occupied their firm place as the judgement of the gods.

Thus on the one hand the ὀργὴ θεοῦ proves to be essentially a mythological concept. But on the other hand it follows from its use as a synonym for the technical term μήνιμα and μῆνις in the aetiological legends or from statements such as that in Apollodo Bibliotheca II.1.3 that there are still in later Greek strong connections with the cult.

Popular belief tends to see in unusual natural phenomena such as pestilence, storm and hail, malformations and illness, the consequences of the ὀργή of the gods and demons (cf. Clement of Alexandria, *Strom.* VI.3.31.1). In Cleonai for instance magicians understand how to avert such catastrophes by sacrifices and magical song. Clement of Alexandria who reports this (*loc. cit.* 2; cf. Plut. *Ser. Num. Pun.* 12 [II.557a-e]), naturally holds to the philosophical opinion: 'the divine is not angry' (*Paed.* I.8.68.3) and censures the Greeks, amongst whom the gods *like an old shrew losing her temper,*[1] *are embittered at what is no injury, as they say* (Hom. *Il.* 9.533-538) *Artemis was wroth with the Aetolians on account of Oeneus* (*Strom.* VII.44.23.2), so that men *in their dealings with beings* (i.e. the gods) *who are so quick to wrath naturally become superstitious and think that whatever happens is a sign and cause of evil* (*Strom.* VII.4.24.1; cf. Tac. *Historiae* II.1). This latter idea indicates a religious attitude which received a particular stamp amongst the Romans from their understanding of the *ira deum.*

3. Ira Deum *amongst the Romans*

At first the Romans admitted extensively into their literature the conceptions of the wrath of the gods as they were described in Greek poetry and mythology

---

[1] But cf. Solon fr. 1.25 f. (Diehl). Cf. p. 5.

from Homer onwards.[1] Similarly the philosophical criticism to which it is subjected reproduces Greek thought and ideas.[2] Furthermore the *revealed wrath of the heavenly beings*, which instigated the transfer of the statue of Serapis from Sinope to Alexandria, originated according to an explicit account in Tacitus (*Historiae* IV.84) in a Hellenistic cult legend. But independently of Greek influence the Romans still had their own original conception of the *ira deum* which had its roots in the peculiar nature of their ancestral *religio*. This is expressed by the belief in evil portents (*prodigia*) in which to Roman thought the wrath of the gods always appears and acts[3] (cf. Livy 5.143). The *ira deum* which is usually provoked by *neglegentia caeremoniarum auspiciorumque* the *neglect of ceremonials and auspices* (Livy 22.9.1) becomes the cause of natural disasters, famine, sickness and epidemics in town and country (Livy 4.9.3). Livy in 40.37.2 writes of a wholesale mortality in Rome in which the *pontifex Maximus* gave orders for rites designed to placate the *ira deum*. In order to exorcise the calamity and to re-establish the *pax deum* (Livy 27.23.4), the good relations with the gods, *piacula irae deum*, the technical term employed, in the shape of *preces*, *vota*, *dona*, *supplicationes* and the like, must be found (Livy 22.9.1; Lucan I.683). The *ira deum* can be recognised by the rites of propitiation as well as by the formalised language as a conception and an expression of the Roman cult. Accordingly although Cicero was aware that philosophy rejected in general

[1] Lucretius, *De Rerum Natura* V.399 ff.; Cicero, *Tusc.* IV.29(63); Virgil, *Aen.*7.305 from Hom. *Il.* 9.533 ff.; *Georgics* III.152 f.; Horace, *Epodi* 10.13 f.; Tac., *Ann.* 3.61.

[2] Lucretius, *De Rerum Natura* VI.753 f.; V.1194 ff.; VI.70 ff.; II.651; Cicero. *Nat. Deor.* I.16 f. (42.5); III.38(91); *Off.* III.102; Sen. *De Ira* II.30.2.

[3] For the following, cf. H. Kleinknecht, 'Laokoon' in Hermes 79 (1944), pp. 82, 108 f.

the wrath of the gods and himself brings out this fact
(p. 5), he admitted into the draft of the laws of his
Utopia concerning the intercourse with the gods, the
regulations to be followed by the augurs and others to
meet the *ira deum* (*De Legibus* II.21); and the universal
rule shall be observed that the impious man should not
dare to placate the *ira deum* with gifts (*loc. cit.* 22),[1]
because the wrath of the deity falls in particular upon
the impious.[2] Just as the gods can be entreated in
prayer to direct their anger against the evil-doer and
the enemy,[3] so the man who swears a solemn oath calls
down upon himself the anger of father Jupiter, of Mars
Gradivus and of the other gods in the event of perjury
(Livy 2.45.15). The *ira deum* which visits him who
scorns the gods, occupies a firm place especially in
cultic legends and tales of miraculous punishment
(Livy 2.36.5, 9.29.11; Tac. *Ann.* 14.22). Piety has often
embellished such reports further, so that the historian
occasionally refrains from expressing an opinion as to
their truth (Livy 8.6.3). In fact amongst the people as
in the army *religio*, i.e. scrupulous attention to hints
from the gods, especially in times of crisis, often became
superstitio, which in its fear immediately interprets fortuitous and natural events as signs of divine wrath (Tac.
Historiae IV.26). Thus for example when the body of
the murdered Britannicus was burned, such a cloud-
burst poured down, that the ordinary people believed
it revealed the *ira deum* (Tac. *Ann.* 13.17).[4] Finally in
Minucius Felix the fact that every conceivable cult was

---

[1] Phrases concerning the wrath of the gods are also to be found
frequently in Cicero's speeches: *Mil.* 86; *Pro. Q. Roscio* 46; *Pro
Caelio* 42; *In Pisonem* 59.

[2] cf. Horace, *Epodi* 10.13 f.; *Carmina* I.3.38 ff.; Tac. *Ann.* I.30.

[3] cf. Livy 9.1.8; Horace, *Epodi* 5.53 f. Cf. also Seneca's censure
of this (*De Ira* II.30.2).

[4] cf. in addition Tac. *Ann.* 1.30 and for this again the philosophical criticism in Sen. *De Ira* II.27.2.

so readily accepted by the Romans in the course of their history was traced back to the fear of the wrath of the gods.[1] This reveals at the same time the evidence for their unique religious feeling, on which the conception of the *ira deum* set a decisive stamp.

But now, since according to Roman ideas the stability of state and government depends essentially on *religio*, the averting of the evil portents and therewith the propitiation of the *ira deum* was the most far-reaching object of public concern. In addition, disastrous happenings in the history of their political life, such as internal discord, class struggles, civil war or mutinies (Tac. *Ann.* 1.39; *Historiae* II.38) are brought particularly into connection with the *ira deum* or *numinum* (cf. Livy 4.9.3). The anger of the gods is seen at work especially in defeats of armies or capture of cities, and in such passages an allusion to it is appropriate to the style of Roman historical writing (Tac. *Ann.* 16.16). The wrath of the gods had a share in bringing about the destruction of Corinth and Carthage,[2] the defeats at Lake Trasimene (Livy 22.9.1) and Cannae[3] and in the Teutoburg Forest,[4] as well as the reign of terror of a Sejanus and of a Nero (Tac. *Ann.* 4.1) or the annihilation of the Capitol in the year A.D. 69 (Tac. *Historiae* IV.54).

Usually a religious offence, neglect of ceremonials and auspices, but also *temeritas* (*rashness*) and *inscitia* (*ignorance*), rouses the wrath of the gods who when they are asked do themselves indicate ways and means of expiation,[5] in fact they order them. The loftiest of such means of expiation and at the same time the pinnacle of old Roman *religio* and *virtus* is the sacrifice of one's own life in the rite of devotion, as it was carried out

---

[1] *Octavius* 7.2 (cf. p. 3).
[2] cf. Cicero, *Nat. Deor.* III.38(91).
[3] Livy 25.6.6; cf. Valerius Maximus I.1.16.
   Dio Cassius 56.24.2.   [5] Livy 22.9.7 f.

for the first time according to the tradition, by the consul of the year 340 B.C., P. Decius Mus, in the decisive battle of the Latin war. Animal sacrifices had been ineffectual in averting the *ira deum*. Then the consul dedicates himself and the hostile army solemnly to death. His form appears to all to wear an aspect more sublime than merely human, 'as though sent from heaven as a sacrifice to propitiate all divine wrath' which therefore falls upon the foes, and overthrows and destroys them (Livy 8.9.10). By the simile here used: *as if he had been sent from heaven*, the voluntary vicarious sacrifice demanded by the angry deity is at once transformed into an act of divine mercy, which evidently itself desires the religious offence to be expiated; for at the height of the crisis a man is sent who turns towards himself all the threats and dangers sent by the gods (Livy 8.10.7)[1] in order that the *pax deum*,[2] the good understanding between gods and men may be restored.

Amongst Roman historians this cultic religious mode of thought attained a historical significance which it never possessed amongst the Greeks. The *ira deum*, always closely connected with the *fatum* becomes fraught with destiny for the whole course of Roman history. In its endless internal discord Tacitus sees the same madness of men and *deum ira* continually at work (*Historiae* II.30), and he brings up this subject again and again because it threatens the existence of Rome itself (cf. *Ann.* 16.16). It is therefore more than a merely poetic

[1] cf. G. Stübler, 'Die Religiosität des Livius,' in Tübinger Beiträge zur Altertumswissenschaft, 35 (1941), pp. 101-201. For the historical truth of the occurrence, cf. F. Altheim, 'Der Opfertod der Decier', in Forschungen und Fortschritte, 17 (1941), pp. 112 f.

[2] This expresses the real antithesis to the concept of *ira deum*; other instances are *deum benignitas* (Tac. *Ann.* 12.45; *Historiae* V.85), *indulgentia numinum* (*Ann.* 13.57), *favor erga nos reorum* (*Germania* 33).

technique of presentation, adopted from that great model, Homer, when in Virgil's *Aeneid*[1] the wrath of the gods appears as the dominant theme and as a driving force in bringing to fulfilment the fate which led Aeneas to Latium (Virgil, *Aen.* 1.2 ff.; cf. 1.130, 5.781). The introduction closes with the question: *Can resentment so fierce dwell in heavenly breasts?* (Virgil, *Aen.* 1.11). Again and again divine beings and human seers point to this wrath of the gods (Virgil, *Aen.* 3.362-366). It has sprung from the Roman world of ideas, as can be inferred from the use of cultic terminology connected with it, from its association with prodigious events and from the rite which in what follows is to implore the *pax deum* (*loc. cit.* 369 ff.). In this matter *ira deum* and *fata* are not to be separated from each other, since they are the negative and positive aspects of one and the same situation. On the one hand Athene announces to Aeneas through the mouth of her priest Nautes: *either what the mighty wrath of the gods portended or what the course of fate demanded* (Virgil, *Aen.* 5.706 f.); on the other hand the wrath of the gods strikes the enemies of the Trojans and thereby makes them understand that[2] *Aeneas is called of fate, guided by heaven's clear will* (11.232 f.). When Aeneas has reached his goal, the god of the river Tiber appears to him in a dream with the consolation and instruction: *the wrath of the gods has abated . . . duly offer prayers to Juno, and with the suppliant's vows vanquish her wrath and her threats* (8.40 f.; cf. Livy 8.33.7). The wrath of the gods, in this case that of Juno, which is appeased and comes to an end here, is none other than the metaphysical expression of the heavy reverses and the more than human opposition[3] with which fate has to contend in working itself out in its temporal, that is to say, in its historical development. Thus Virgil has

---

[1] cf. also Petronius *Satirae* 139; cf. 134.
[2] cf. Livy 36.6.   [3] cf. Virgil *Aen.* 7.315.

filled the prescribed epic form in the poetic tradition of the Greeks with the religious content of a genuinely Roman point of view, which by its avowed application to history represents a new and essential feature in the classical conception of the wrath of the gods.

II. THE WRATH OF MAN AND THE WRATH OF GOD IN THE OLD TESTAMENT

1. *The Hebrew terms*

HEBREW is very rich in expressions each of which describes a particular feature of anger:

(a) the most usual term is '*ap* which is to be derived from '*ānap* to *be angry*, originally no doubt to *snort*[1] and hence may have the fundamental meaning of *snorter*.[2] From this there follows the meaning *nose*, in the dual *nose, nostrils*. The OT considers the nose not so much an organ of smell (thus in Amos iv.10; Ps. cxv.6), as an 'organ of anger', when God's anger is kindled, *ḥārāh* '*ap*, smoke goes up from his nostrils (Ps. xviii.9). '*Ap* and the much more rare dual form[3] are found about 210 times in the OT—about 170 times for divine and 40 times for human anger. The combination *ḥārāh* '*ap* is met with in the most diverse writings of the OT, but chiefly in the earlier sources of the Pentateuch and the historical books.[4] The verb '*ānap* occurs only 14 times, 8 times in the Qal and 6 times in the Hithpaʿel; it is used only of God. Although one might wish to deduce from this a specific usage of the verb, the employment of '*ap* and its dual form also for human anger and the rare occurrence of the verb suggests the need for caution.

(b) The most frequent synonym for '*ap* is *ḥēmāh* which is to be derived from the root *yāḥam* to *be hot*, to *be ardent*. It denotes also the glow of wine in Hos. vii.5,

---

[1] L. Köhler, *Lexicon Veteris Testamenti libros* (1948 ff.), 70.

[2] *op. cit.* 75; or is the noun primary and the verb derived from it?

[3] It is found for anger, e.g. in Exod. xv.8 and Prov. xxx.33, but especially in the phrases *slow to anger* ('*erek* '*appaim*) and *impatient* (*qᵉṣar* '*appaim*).   [4] For *ḥārāh*, cf. the detailed comments below.

the agitation of the spirit in Ezek. iii.14, the poison of
the serpents in Deut. xxxii.24; Ps. lviii.5, cxl.4(3), and
the poisoned arrows in Job vi.4; but much the most
often (115 times) the anger and fury of God (about 90
times), as well as that of man (about 25 times).

(c) The MT uses the term *ḥārōn* exclusively for the
anger of God; it is found 39 times in all,[1] and in 33 of
these passages in the combination *ḥᵃrōn 'ap*. On the
other hand the related word *ḥᵒrī* which occurs only 6
times and always in the combination *ḥᵒrī 'ap* is used
both for the anger of God (twice) and for that of man
(4 times). Both nouns are to be derived from *ḥārāh*
which is used in the Qal only with regard to anger (of
God and man) and appears thus 80 times; in the derived forms, it has the meaning of being *eager*, to *inveigh*.
Its original meaning is probably to be *kindled*, to *glow*;
thus the nouns in combination with *'ap* denote the
kindling of anger and more generally the heat of anger.
Owing to the fact that the Qal of *ḥārāh* refers exclusively to anger,[2] *ḥārōn* must be interpreted as
anger also in the few passages where it is found without
'ap.

(d) *'ebrāh* meaning *anger* is not to be derived from the
frequently used root *'ābar* I to *flow over*, to *cross over*, to
step over which begins in Arabic with 'ayin,[3] but from
'ābar II the less common root, which is *ĝabira* in Arabic.
Its meaning must be assumed to be to *bear ill-will*, to
be angry. *'ebrāh*, *anger*, is used in 24 passages with reference to God, in 6 passages referring to man; the verb
'ābar II occurs in the OT only in the Hithpaʻel and then

---

[1] Ps. viii.10 and Jer. xxv.38 are not counted in this, since the
text is uncertain.

[2] *ḥārāh* is found 50 times with *'ap*, 26 times with a dative of the
person, and in some other combinations (cf. Gen. xxxi.35, xlv.5).

[3] From this root is to be derived *'ebrāh* I *arrogance*, *excess* (Is.
xvi.6; Jer. xlviii.30(29); Prov. xxi.24).

with the meaning to *lose one's temper*, to *be angry* (said of
God and man, altogether 7 times).

(*e*) The verb *qāṣap* (occurring 28 times in the Qal[1]),
from which is derived *qeṣep*, has perhaps the original
meaning of to *break out*, from which to *let fly*, to *be angry*
is easily explained.[2] Whilst the verb is used both for
God and men being angry, the noun is used quite pre-
ponderantly of God's anger (26 times) and only twice
(Eccl. v.16 and Est. i.18, hence in very late writings) of
the anger, or vexation of a man.[3]

(*f*) From the verb *zāʿam* (12 times in the OT)
which means to *let fly at*, to *scold*, to *be angry with*, but
also to *cast a spell on*, to *curse*, was formed the noun *zaʿam*
which no doubt originally in accordance with this
means *anger* with its expression by invective in view.[4]
So in Isa. xxx.27 it can be said of the lips of Yahweh.

In 5 of the 6 passages which use it with regard to
God,[5] the verb clearly means his *anger* and even in the
6th this sense is quite likely (Num. xxiii.8) even though
here the meaning to *curse* is not excluded; in the 5
passages where it is used with regard to a man the
meaning to be angry seems to me nowhere to be required.[6] In Mic. vi.10 the passive participle of the Qal
is used of a thing, the accursed scanty ephah. Thus
the verb with the meaning to be angry is only used for
divine anger. The employment of the noun *zaʿam*

---

[1] Hiphʿil (5 times) to *provoke to anger*.

[2] Hos. x.7 uses *qeṣep* in the concrete sense (*wood shaving* or *foam*);
does this perhaps come from another root (cf. Gesenius-Buhl)?

[3] It is in any case (unlike the verb) found almost exclusively in
late writings, especially in P and in the Chronicler (but cf. II
Kings iii.27); for its absolute use, cf. below, p. 24.

[4] Köhler's (cf. p. 14 n. 1) rendering by to *cast a spell on, scold*
(262) is too restricted; the same applies to his translation of *zaʿam*
merely by *curse*; cf. Isa. x.5 where *zaʿam* occurs as a parallel to *'ap*.

[5] Isa. lxvi.14; Zech. i.12; Mal. i.4; Ps. vii.12(11); Prov. xxii.14.

[6] Num. xxiii. 7 parallel to *'ārar*; Num. xxiii.8; Prov. xxiv.24
parallel to *qābab*; Prov. xxv.23; Dan. xi.30.

agrees with this, for in the 22 passages in which it occurs it denotes without exception the anger of God.[1] Moreover verb and noun are met with only in poetic texts and in fact principally in those of later times. A special usage of *za'am* is to be found in the apocalyptic writings where perhaps it can denote the *time of anger*; cf. Isa. xxvi.20; Dan. viii.19, xi.36 (cf. p. 44).

(*g*) The root *zā'ap*, related to *za'am*, is represented considerably less often. In the four passages in which the verb *zā'ap* occurs (original meaning *rage, storm?*), it is used of persons and things and only in Prov. xix.3; II Chron. xxvi.19 does it mean to *be angry*; the verbal adjective *zā'ēp* sullen, angry is found in I Kings xx.43, xxi.4. The noun *za'ap* is used with reference to God twice, to men 4 times and figuratively of the raging of the sea in Jon. i.15; like the verb *zā'ap* (except for Gen. xl.6) it is used only in post-exilic passages.

(*h*) *kā'as* in the Qal (6 times) means to *be annoyed*, to *be resentful*, to *be angry*; in the Pi'el (twice) and the Hiph'il (nearly 50 times) it has the causative meaning of to *offend*, to *vex*, to *provoke to anger*, where it is almost always God who is the object of the provocation. The Hiph'il is used principally in Deuteronomy, in the historical books which have undergone Deuteronomic revision (Judges and Kings) and in passages of Jeremiah handed down with this same revision, when it is a question of Israel arousing God's anger by apostasy and the worship of idols. The noun *ka'as*—in the book of Job always in the form *ka'as* (cf. Job v.2, vi.2, x.17,

---

[1] This applies also to Jer. xv.17 (cf. vi.11). In Hos. vii.16 there is no doubt a textual error (cf. LXX); according to T. H. Robinson, *Die Zwölf kleinen Propheten* (1938), p. 30, *za'am* here means perhaps as much as *insolence*. *za'am Yahweh* is not found anywhere but *za'am* with the pronominal suffix as applied to Yahweh occurs 11 times; elswhere it is used absolutely (with or without the article) e.g. Isa. xxvi.20; Dan. viii.19; but also in Ezek. xxii.24; Ps. lxxviii.49), most characteristically in the later period.

xvii.7)—is used 8 times of God, 17 times of man and means *vexation, displeasure* (*anger?*).[1]

(*i*) Since the verb *rāgaz* means to *become excited, disturbed*—in the Hiphʻil also once (Job xii.6) to *provoke to anger*—the far more rare noun is likely to denote *rage, agitation*, even *anger*; this shows a restriction of meaning, as compared with the verb which can also be used in the sense of *being happily excited* (Jer. xxxiii.9). *rōgez* occurs only 7 times, and then with a figurative meaning for the agitations of life and the raging of man against God; only in Hab. iii.2 is it to be understood of the anger of God. The verb occurs about 40 times in writings of all the OT periods, the noun only in late passages.

(*k*) *rūaḥ*[2] can hardly be called a proper term for anger, although the word approaches the sphere of anger in the shade of meaning of to *snort*; cf. *qeṣar rūaḥ* paralleled by *ʼerek ʼappaim*[3] in Prov. xiv.29.[4] In Job iv.9 *rūaḥ* is found in association with *ʼap*.

2. *The wrath of man in the Old Testament*

Although the same terms are used in the main for divine and human wrath, there are considerable material differences between the two conceptions. We will treat first the presentation of human wrath in the OT. Usually those who display it are individuals—Israelites[5] and non-Israelites[6]—occasionally also groups

---

[1] Eccl. ii.23, v.16, vii.3, xi.10 *vexation*.

[2] cf. *Spirit of God* (1960) in this series, pp. 1-7.

[3] cf. above, p. 14 n. 3.

[4] cf. Isa. xxx.28 (God's snorting with rage), xxv.4; Prov.xvi.32, xxix.11 (of men).

[5] e.g. Moses in Exod. xxxii.19; Samuel in I Sam. xv.11; David in II Sam. vi.8; Uzziah in II Chron. xxvi.19.

[6] Potiphar in Gen. xxxix.19; Pharaoh in Gen. xl.2; Naaman in II Kings v.12; Sanballat in Neh. iv.1; Haman in Est. iii.5.

of people and nations,[1] and also their rulers.[2] In the case of the nations it is their extreme wrath in war, their furious rage, against the people of God[3] which is threatening (Amos i.11; Isa. li.13; Ezek. xxxv.11), though it is declared to be ineffectual against the protection of Yahweh (Isa. vii.4; Ps. cxxix.3).

i. *Against other men.* The wrath of man is directed mainly against other men.[4] Human wrath is just and godly whenever it is aroused not merely in order to preserve individual rights.[5] Thus the wrath of David—to whom Nathan appealed as the highest judge—is kindled against the rich man in the story (II Sam. xii.5), or that of Nehemiah against the abused in Jerusalem (Neh. v.6); cf. also Saul's wrath against the Ammonites, which is attributed directly to the 'spirit of Yahweh' (I Sam. xi.6). The position is similar in the case of Shechem's assault on Dinah, which arouses the wrath of her brothers who take a cruel revenge (Gen. xxxiv.7),[6] and again in that of David's wrath against Amnon when he had violated Tamar (II Sam. xiii.21), although in these last two passages the disinterested motive of the wrath is not so clearly evident, for here the honour and existence of the clan are at stake. On

[1] Commanders of the Philistines in I Sam. xxix.7; the enemies of the righteous in Ps. vii.7; Edom in Amos i.11; Babylon in Isa. li.13.

[2] Nebuchadnezzar in Dan. iii.13; Ahasuerus in Est. i.12.

[3] Or against other nations in Isa. xiv.6; Dan. xi.44.

[4] Once only is there any note of wrath or resentment against an animal (Balaam's ass) in Num. xxii.27.

[5] The passage in the psalms (Ps. iv.5(4) cited in Eph. iv.26) ὀργίζεσθε καὶ μὴ ἁμαρτάνετε can hardly belong here; it does not have in view the possibility of a just wrath, but utters a warning lest the rising resentment become a sin (of word or deed).

[6] It is interesting to note that in Jacob's blessing the wrath of these brothers of Dinah is condemned (Gen. xlix.3-7); perhaps in fact because it was uncontrolled (H. Gunkel, *Genesis* ([5]1922) *ad loc.*).

the other hand special mention must be made of that just and godly wrath which has to do with the defence of Yahweh's cause directly in face of the infringement of his claim to sovereignty, of lack of reverence for his holiness. Thus Moses becomes wrathful with the Israelites' want of faith in God (Exod. xvi.20), with their apostasy at the mountain of God (Exod. xxxii.19, 23), with their sparing the Midianite women which had been forbidden (Num. xxxi.14), and concerning a cultic offence (Lev. x.16). There is a similar reason for the wrath of Elisha (II Kings xiii.19)[1] and of Elihu (Job xxxii.2, 3, 5). But above all the prophets must be mentioned here as those who proclaim God's wrath and amongst them in particular Jeremiah and Ezekiel.[2] Jeremiah is obliged to say of himself: 'Therefore I am full of the wrath of the Lord' (vi.11; cf. xv.17) and this wrath of God is heard in many of his words as well in those of the other prophets against the people of God and against foreign nations.[3]

There seem to be merely selfish grounds for the wrath of the man who feels himself to be injured in his real or supposedly justifiable claim.[4] Thus, for example, Cain is angry with Abel in Gen. iv.5; Esau with Jacob in Gen. xxvii.44 f.; Balak with Balaam in Num. xxiv.10; Saul with Jonathan in I Sam. xx.30; the tribes of Israel

---

[1] cf. also Elijah's action against the prophets of Baal (without the technical term for wrath) in I Kings xviii.40.

[2] cf. p. 28 n. 2, 3.

[3] It is true that at times the blaze of wrath seems here to be fanned by human and national passion which is in danger of identifying its own nation's cause with that of God (particularly in post-exilic prophecy).

[4] Here the dividing line between wrath and ill-will is often fluid; in particular passages it is not a question of the natural violent outburst of wrath, but of the expression of sullen ill-will against an unexpected and unwelcome happening (as in Gen. xxx.2, xxxi.35 f., xliv.18; I Sam. xxix.4; I Kings xxi.4; II Kings v.12).

with Judah in II Sam. xix.43; Pharaoh with his servants in Gen. xl.1 f.; Potiphar with Joseph in Gen. xxxix.19 and Ahasuerus with the queen Vashti in Est. i.12. Again when a man of God utters demands or threats, the wrath of the man concerned is kindled[1]; cf. Ahab when threatened by Elijah in I Kings xx.43; Asa when reproached by the seer in II Chron. xvi.10; Uzziah when forbidden by the priests in II Chron. xxvi.19.

ii. *Against God.* Man's wrath or ill-will can be directed against God himself if his dealings appear to him enigmatic and incomprehensible and he cannot reconcile them with God's justice; e.g. Samuel when Saul is rejected in I Sam. xv.11, David when Uzzah is killed in II Sam. vi.8, Job in view of his undeservedly hard fate in Job x.2 f.; xviii.4 and Jonah with regard to God's mercy to Nineveh in Jon. iv.1, 4, 9.[2] Basically the wrath of the 'righteous' because of the good fortune of the 'ungodly' is directed also against God and his authority (Ps. xxxvii.1, 7 f.; Prov. iii.31 f.).[3]

iii. *Critical assessment.* The Wisdom literature alone criticises human anger.[4] The wise men in Proverbs measure it in part by utilitarian standards in accordance with the general attitude of Wisdom thought. Wrath is dangerous because it produces trouble and has bad consequences (Prov. vi.34, xv.1, xvi.14, xix.19, xxvii.4); therefore it is to be avoided and calmed down (Prov. xv.18, xxii.24, xxix.8, 11). A warning is also given against the intelligible wrath about the good fortune of the ungodly who will receive their punishment

[1] It is in fact directed against God himself, by whom these men know that they are sent.

[2] The LXX renders *ḥārāh* in these passages with ἀθυμεῖν in I and II Sam. and with λυπεῖσθαι in Jon. iv.

[3] In Prov. iii.31b note *his ways*; and for *choose* read *be angry at* (Hithpaʿel of *ḥārāh*). Cf. LXX and Kittel BH.

[4] Lev. xix.18 forbids vindictiveness or resentment.

later (Prov. xxix.19 f.; Ps. xxxvii.7-9). Hence he who is slow to anger is praised as being truly wise (Prov. xiv.29, xv.18, xvi.32; Eccles. vii.8), whilst the hot-tempered man[1] is condemned as a fool (Prov. iv.17, 29).

The wise of course know too that the anger of men leads to wrong doing (Prov. xiv.17, xxix.22); the letter of James which is closely connected with the Wisdom literature takes up this theme in i.20: ὀργὴ γὰρ ἀνδρὸς δικαιοσύνην θεοῦ οὐκ ἐργάζεται (cf. p. 80). The contrast appearing in Proverbs 'the angry man—the wise man' is rooted not in Greek philosophy, but rather in Egyptian wisdom,[2] where the fool can be called simply the hot-head.[3] Job's anger against God is most severely condemned by his friends because by it he not only harms himself (xviii.4), but is 'doing away with the fear of God' (xv.4) and calling God's justice in question (viii.2 f., xi.2 f. et passim). God's speeches acknowledge formally that this view is right, but substantiate it on a much deeper level in Job xxxviii ff. and Job repents that he spoke to God irreverently in anger and humbles himself (xlii.6).

3. The wrath of God in the Old Testament

i. Discussion of the terms

In the OT the terms for wrath denote divine wrath considerably more often than human wrath.[4] Some of them are used in the OT literature exclusively for the wrath of God, such as ḥārōn or ḥᵃrōn 'ap, zaʿam and the

---

[1] Similarly Prov. xxii.24 and Prov. xxix.22.

[2] cf. J. Fichtner, Die altorientalische Weisheit in ihrer israelitischen Ausprägung (1933), pp. 20 f.

[3] For example in Amenemope: 'Do not consort with the hot-head.' ANET, p. 423, DOTT, p. 180; cf. Hempel, Althebräische Literatur (1930), p. 51.

[4] Nouns for wrath are used about 375 times for divine, about 80 times for human wrath.

verb ʾānap, others predominantly, namely qeṣep[1] and
ʿebrāh, whilst ʾap and ḥēmāh and the less frequent zaʿap
(and rōgez) are employed for human and divine wrath.
Possibly ḥārōn or ḥᵃrōn ʾap[2] and zaʿam[3] were in fact re-
served to reference to divine wrath in the current usage
of the spoken language, though the precise evidence of
usage is too scanty for a reliable verdict on this. It is
significant that combinations of the terms for wrath are
used only to denote divine wrath.[4] Apart from compound phrases ḥᵃrōn ʾap (33 times),[5] zaʿap ʾap (Isa.
xxx.30), zaʿam ʾap (Lam. ii.6) and ʿebrōt ʾap (Job xl.11),
syndetic combinations of two or even three of the terms
are found: ʾap and ḥēmāh (about 15 times), other combinations in Isa. xiii.9, Ps. cii.11(10), Deut. xxix.27
(similarly in Jer. xxi.5, xxxii.37) and Ps. lxxviii.49; cf.
also Deut. ix.19; Ezek. v.15, xiii.13. The piling up of
words, amongst which except in Ps. cii.11(10) the chief
term is always ʾap or ḥᵃrōn ʾap, brings out the difference
in quality between human and divine wrath by giving
an impressive and vivid picture of the mighty pressure
of God's holy wrath, which no one can resist (Ps.
lxxvi.8; Neh. i.6). The combinations of a word for
wrath with the designations for God contain almost
exclusively the divine name Yahweh. ʾap, ḥēmāh, ʿebrāh
and qeṣep are combined more than 50 times with Yahweh.[6] ʾap ᵉlōhīm is found only twice, namely in Ps.
lxxviii.31—in the Elohist psalter (Ps. xlii-lxxxix) where
Elohim is substituted for Yahweh[7]—and in Num. xxii.22

---

[1] The verb qāṣap is used for divine and human wrath.

[2] Perhaps to make a conscious distinction from ḥᵃrē ʾap.

[3] Similarly also the verb zāʿam.

[4] The occurrence of synonyms in the parallel members of verses
are not included in this (40 times, of which only 3 times of human
wrath).

[5] Is found 4 times for human wrath.

[6] About 40 of these are ʾap Yahweh.

[7] The basic passage in Num. xi.33 has ʾap Yahweh.

where there is textual evidence for the reading *Yahweh*[1];
in Ezra x.14 we have the phrase *our God*, practically
identical with *Yahweh* combined with *ḥᵃrōn 'aƥ* and
finally in Job xxi.20 *ḥᵃmat šaddai* which is not surprising
in the dialogue in Job where the name Yahweh is
avoided. The consistent combination of the nouns of
wrath with Yahweh, the God of the covenant, is of
considerable theological importance; it shows that the
idea of wrath is to a large extent connected with the
faith of the covenant.[2]

In later times there is an evident effort to weaken or
even to break too close a connection of God with wrath.
This is brought out in the usage by the absolute use of
the word wrath, which we find especially in the case of
qeṣeƥ occasionally in the post-exilic period, amongst the
Priestly writers in particular. In P *qeṣeƥ Yahweh* never
occurs; once we read *wrath (qeṣeƥ) has gone forth from
Yahweh* (Num. xvi.46 [Heb. xvii.11]), otherwise only
qeṣeƥ (Num. i.53, xviii.5; Josh. ix.20, xxii.20, probably
also xxii.18[3] and Lev. x.6)[4]. The Chronicler indeed has
qeṣeƥ Yahweh twice (II Chron. xxix.9, xxxii.26), but
beside it a *qeṣeƥ* by itself (I Chron. xxvii.24; II Chron.
xix.2,[5] xix.10, xxiv.18, xxxii.25). He replaces the
wrath of Yahweh which, according to II Sam. xxiv.1,
incites David to number the people, by Satan in I
Chron. xxi.1. It is true that in both authors we also find
'aƥ Yahweh, but in the Chronicler chiefly in the material
taken from older sources. What is peculiar to them
is the absolute usage of the term for wrath and

---

[1] 1 MS. of the MT, the Samaritan, LXX (F and N), (Targ. Onkelos).

[2] Moreover there is no term for the wrath of God in Genesis.

[3] Following LXX, Syr. Targ. (cf. verse 20); M. Noth, *Das Buch Josua* (1938) *ad loc.* disagrees with this; he now considers Josh. xxii.9-34 to be a 'very late isolated addition to the book of Joshua' (*Überlieferungsgeschichtliche Studien* (1943), p. 232.)

[4] cf. LXX.   [5] In this passage with *from Yahweh*.

consequently this must be noted. Quite seldom, and also in later times only, we find other expressions for wrath used without direct reference to Yahweh[1]; cf. Ezek. vii.12: *wrath (ḥārōn) is upon all their multitude*[2]; II Chron. xxviii.13: *fierce wrath (ḥᵃrōn 'ap) is upon Israel* and Neh. xiii.18: *you bring more wrath (ḥārōn) upon Israel.*[3] Again in Isa. lxiii.5 the wrath of Yahweh appears strangely dissociated from Yahweh: *my wrath (ḥēmāh) upheld me,* but as the following verse shows, these words do not go further than a poetical personification.[4]

ii. *The objects of divine wrath*

The conception of God's wrath in the OT receives its particular stamp from the fact that basically Israel has to do with only one God[5] and thus the outlet into the pantheon and the world of demons[6] is barred. There is the further fact that the approach to this God involves a particular relationship established by his holy righteousness and electing love. Thus for the godly men of the old covenant the source of the wrath is not an unknown

[1] J. Böhmer, 'Zorn', ZAW, NF. 3 (1926), pp. 320-322, mentions a profusion of other examples of the independent usage of terms for wrath which do not concern us here.

[2] The words are missing in LXX(B); they occur (with *my wrath*) also in verse 14.

[3] J. Boehmer's thesis (cf. previous note), p. 321 that an original belief in 'demons which had not yet been subdued and absorbed by the supreme deity' shimmers through the absolute usage of the terms for wrath is already refuted by the late appearance of this employment of the terms for wrath.

[4] For za'am used absolutely, cf. p. 17, n. 1.

[5] cf. on the other hand, e.g. M. Jastrow, *Die Religion Babyloniens und Assyriens* I (1905), pp. 362, 477-479; S. H. Hooke, *Babylonian and Assyrian Religion* (1953, 1962), pp. 12-38; in the OT only in II Kings iii.27 is a direct mention made of the wrath of another god, Chemosh of the Moabites.

[6] TWNT II, pp. 10 ff.; cf. F. Baumgärtel, *Die Eigenart der alttestamentlichen Frömmigkeit* (1932), p. 63.

deity or even a feeling of the power of fate, but an 'unmistakable definite divine person'.[1] This does not mean that thereby the irrational would be banished from faith in God—this will become clear when we examine the conception of divine wrath more closely—but that the men of the OT, as they became aware of their faith and came to terms with life, found themselves, through their survey of their past history, through their attitude to the present and as they looked into the future, directed along one path alone and met there, not a dark problematic force, but the will of Yahweh like that of a person, with whom it is important to come to terms. The personal quality of the OT conception of God conditions particularly the 'anthropopathic' manner of speaking about wrath, but it gives it also its impressive vitality.[2] The danger of obliterating the dividing line between God and man by excessive anthropopathism is averted because the godly man in the OT had a strong sense of distance with regard to his God[3] and a deep insight into the nature of the divine wrath. This is what differentiates it from human wrath which is rooted predominantly in the tyrannical ego of man.[4]

To proclaim God's wrath is in the OT not the same as to describe the divine act of judgement[5]; this denotes not only an action but a vital process in God himself, 'an emotional disturbance' of God.[6] Now of course in so far as this disturbance does not affect the being of

[1] G. Quell, in *Lord* in this series, p. 44.

[2] cf. W. Eichrodt, *Theologie* I, pp. 98-100 (E.T. (1960), pp. 210 ff.)

[3] cf. J. Hempel, *Gott und Mensch im AT* (1936), 198, pp. 267 f.

[4] For the 'godly, just wrath' of man, cf. above p. 19.

[5] It is true that Yahweh's wrath in action acquires a visible form when he judges; cf. wrath and judgement in Ezek. v.15; Mic. vii.9; Ps. vii.7; wrath and vengeance: Ezek. xxiv.8; Nah. i.2.

[6] F. Weber, p. 11.

God himself,[1] but enters into relationship with the being established by him outside himself, with the world and its powers, those passages of the OT which speak of God's wrath, rightly raise the question at what targets it is directed.

(a) In the first place it is Israel itself at which the wrath of Yahweh is aimed. Already when the covenant is being made, he threatens each one who might approach Yahweh's holiness too closely (Exod. xix. JE), and in the history of the period in the wilderness it plays a significant role both with the Yahwist and the Elohist[2] as well as in Deuteronomy and the Priestly writings.[3] Similarly he intervenes repeatedly in the history of the people from the conquest (cf. Josh. vii. JE(?), xxii.20P) down to the exile (I Sam. vi.19, xv, xxviii.18; II Sam. vi.7, xxiv.1). The Deuteronomic survey of history has presented this period entirely from the point of view of divine wrath ever aroused afresh (cf. pp. 38 f.), and the Chronicler's historical work too has something to say about it (I Chron. xiii.10, xxvii.24; II Chron. xix.2, xxiv.18, xxix.8), as do also the historical psalms (e.g. lxxviii.31, cvi.32).[4] These passages display—especially in the earlier period—the collective involvement of the individual within the totality of God's people. God's wrath is directed against the individual in his particular function amongst the people of God, e.g. (against Moses (Exod. iv.14; Deut. i.37), Aaron (Deut. ix.20); Miriam

---

[1] Such a possibility is completely alien to the OT way of thinking.

[2] Exod. xxxii; Num. xi.1, 10, 33, xii.9, xiii.25, xiv.38, xxv.3, 4.

[3] Deut. i.34, 37, ix.8, 19 f. Num. xvii. 11,xviii.5, xxv.7-13, xxxii. 10-14, Lev. x.6.

[4] cf. also the exhortations of Deut. (vi.15, vii.4, xi.17, xxix.19 ff.) or the corresponding sections from the Priestly tradition (Lev. xxvi.28; Num. i.53; Josh. xxii.18; II Chron. xix.10). It is very significant that in the legal corpora of the Pentateuch there are only sporadic cases of the threatening wrath of God being made the motive for obedience (Exod. xxii.23; Lev. xxvi.20).

(Num. xii.9), Nadab and Abihu (Lev. x.6) and against kings and prophets (I Sam. xv; II Kings xxiii.26; II Chron. xxix.8; Jer. xxi.1-7). On the other hand in his wrath his judgement strikes the whole people on account of the sin of individuals (Josh. vii, Achan's theft, II Sam. xxiv, David's census). In the later period this collective bond is relaxed (cf. Ps. vi.2(1), xxvii.9, xxxviii.2(1)).

Amongst the prophets, it was especially those active before the exile who made the onset of Yahweh's wrath against his people the central subject of their message, even if they—as, e.g. Amos—do not all employ for it the term wrath.[1] Their conflict is with the false security of the people founded on their consciousness of being chosen and felt to be protected from wrathful condemnation (Amos iii.2, v.18; Hos. xiii.9-11; Isa. v.18 f., xxviii.14-22; Mic. iii.11; Zeph. ii.2; Jer. vii.4, xxviii. 1-17; Ezek. v.13, xvi.38). Amongst them Jeremiah[2] and Ezekiel[3] can actually be described as prophets of Yahweh's wrath against his people. The prophets during and after the exile do indeed see this as the consequence of Yahweh's wrath[4] and no longer like their predecessors proclaim the annihilating onslaught of his wrath on the people of God; but yet they are aware—particularly after the return—that Yahweh's wrath still rests on the people (Hag. i. 5-11; Zech. i.3, 12) or threatens it anew (Joel, Isa. liv.8); we hear the same in the laments of this period Ps. lxxiv.1-8, lxxxv.4, 6).

[1] It may be stated as a matter of principle that we make use in the first place of passages which employ the technical terms for wrath, but occasionally refer also to passages in which the concept of wrath appears without the corresponding technical terms.

[2] Jer. iv.4, 8, 26, vii.20, 29, xvii.4, xxxii.31, xxxvi.7 *et passim*.

[3] Ezek. v.15, vi.12, vii.8, viii.15, xiv.19, xvi.38, xx.8 *et passim*. cf. A. Ruegg, RE³ 21, 720.

[4] Isa. xlii.25, xlvii.6, li.17, lx.10; Zech. i.2, 13.

(*b*) The nations and their rulers are objects of God's wrath as well as Israel. The prophetic threats are directed against them in the so-called 'oracles of the nations' in the books of Amos, Isaiah, Jeremiah and Ezekiel and in the prophecies of Zephaniah, Obadiah, Nahum, Habakkuk and Joel and also in the book of Jonah.[1] The prophets of the exilic and post-exilic period in particular announce the wrath of God against the nations (Isa. xiii.3, 5, 9, 13, xxx.27, lix.18, lx.3, 6, lxvi.14; Jer. l.13, 15, li.45; Ezek. xxv.4, xxx.15; Jonah iii.9 *et passim*.[2] The Psalms too which speak of the final victory of Yahweh and his Anointed threaten the peoples with God's wrath (Ps. ii.5, 12, cx.5). When he breaks forth in the days to come, all the earth (cf. Deut. xxxii.22), all mankind will be affected by it (Jer. x.10; Isa. xiii.9, 11; Zeph. iii.8), just as in the days of old his condemnation struck all men (Gen. iii, vi-viii, xi).

iii. *Divine wrath in action*

The description of the divine wrath in action, of its effects and instruments, must take account of very varied material in the OT tradition.[3] One thing is common to the diverse ways in which God's wrath is shown at work; where it threatens or takes action, the very existence of him who is struck is at stake; in other words, when the existence of a man of the old covenant is threatened, he becomes aware of the wrath of his God.

The annihilating might of God's wrath and his irresistible power are displayed in the metaphors and pictorial phrases used for what that wrath brings about.

---

[1] cf. H. Gressmann, *Der Messias* (1929), pp. 97-148.

[2] Sometimes the names of particular nations are specified, sometimes only 'the nations' in general are spoken of.

[3] cf. II Sam. vi.7, xxiv.1 with Jeremiah's sermon on wrath or Num. i.53, xvii.11 with the experience of the divine wrath in the book of Job.

Here a distinction must be made between metaphors which are taken from a field remote from the sphere of wrath and illustrate a typical feature of the occurrence of wrath, and those descriptions used not only as metaphors but in addition representing the way in which the divine wrath at work actually makes its appearance. This applies to the commonest metaphor of God's wrath which expresses in a particularly vivid manner its devastating effect, the metaphor of fire. When Yahweh's holiness is violated, then his wrath is kindled,[1] a fire flares up in his nostrils (Jer. xv.14, xvii.4; cf. Isa. lxv.5), and smoke rises from them (Ps. xviii.9),[2] his tongue is *like a devouring fire* in Isa. xxx.27.[3] The blazing and consuming fire is by no means only a metaphor for God in anger, but it also represents the wrath actually at work: *the breath of Yahweh, like a stream of brimstone, kindles it (tōpheth)* in Isa. xxx.33; cf. Deut. xxxii.22; Ezek. xx.31. The use of metaphors and actual descriptions of the fire of wrath can also pass directly into each other; cf. Ezek. xxi.31 [Heb. 36 f.]; Isa. xxx.27-33. This shows to how small an extent these biblical statements are intended to be metaphors (in our sense). Something similar to the metaphor of fire applies to that of the storm which represents the destructive power of wrath, even though it occurs more rarely than the former in connection with wrath (Jer. xxx.23; cf. Isa. xxx.30; Ps. lxxxiii.16[4] and also Isa. ii.6-22). Akin to the conception of the storm of wrath is that of Yahweh snorting in wrath, which lies behind the use of the word

[1] Usually *ḥārāh*, also *bāʿar* in Ps. ii.12(11), *yāṣat* in II Kings xxii.13 and *yāqad* in Isa. lxv.5.

[2] In Deut. xxix.19(20) and in Ps. lxxiv.1 smoke actually takes the place of wrathfulness.

[3] cf. also the etymology of *ḥārāh* and cf. p. 15.

[4] The LXX has significantly rendered with ὀργή both *storm* (Ps. lxxxiii.15 [LXX, lxxxii.16]) and also *storm* and *tempest* (Jer. xxx.23 [LXX, xxxvii.23]).

rūaḥ (cf. p. 18) and can be seen in the etymology of *'ānap* and *'ap* (cf. p. 14).

The wrath of God, in addition to being represented as heat, fire and storm, has another description, namely as a liquid. This occurs in the metaphor of *emptying out* and *drinking* the wrath. God pours out his wrath over the people of God and the foreign nations as water is poured out in Hos. v.10; cf. Jer. x.25; Ps. lxix.24(25) and especially Ezek. vii.8, xiv.19, xx.8 *et passim*. The metaphor of pouring out can be combined with that of fire: cf. Nah. i.6; Lam. ii.4 and in parallel verses or verse members in Ezek. xxi.31 [Heb. 36], xxii.31. It is impossible to decide whether the thought here is of representations of fire and brimstone (Ezek. xxxviii.22) or of streams of pitch (cf. Isa. xxx.33, xxxiv.9), or whether the piling up of metaphors is intended to make vivid the greatness and horror of the judgement of wrath. On the other hand the phrase about drinking the wrath as it occurs in Job xxi.20[1] and especially in the conception of the wine of wrath in Jer. xxv.15[2] and of the cup of wrath in Isa. li.17, 22; Jer. xxv.15 (cf. TWNT III, p. 168; V, p. 166)[3] is pure metaphor. It brings impressively before our eyes the fact that the wrath is inescapable and must be endured to the full.[4] The prophet offering the cup of wrath in Jer. xxv.15-28 calls up irrevocably the judgement of wrath on Jerusalem and the nations.[5]

[1] *Let him drink of the wrath of the Almighty.*

[2] *Wine of wrath* (*ḥēmāh*) occurs only here; the words are sometimes considered to be a gloss. But the LXX (τοῦ οἴνου τοῦ ἀρκάτου) tells against this; did it read *ḥemer* (*fermenting wine*) instead of *ḥēmāh*?

[3] The LXX renders *cup of wrath* (*ḥēmāh*) in Isa. li.7, 22 with τὸ ποτήριον (or τὸ κόνδυ) τοῦ θυμοῦ; in Rev. xiv.10 τὸ ποτήριον τῆς 'οργῆς αὐτοῦ appears with ὁ οἶνος τοῦ θυμοῦ.

[4] In Isa. li.17 *thou hast drunk to the dregs.*

[5] The metaphor of the winepress of wrath is also used once (Isa. lxiii.1-6).

The nations appear as the weapons of the wrathful
God or as the instruments of his chastisement when they
are spoken of as the *weapons of his indignation* (*za'am*) in
Isa. xiii.5; Jer. l.25[1] and also as a *rod of anger* (*'ap*) or
staff of fury (*za'am*) in Isa. x.5.[2] In this vivid metaphor
is summed up the conception current throughout the
whole OT that God can let his wrath be carried out by
earthly powers. Beside it there appears the more
abstract notion that he employs his arm as the instrument of his wrath in Isa. ix.12(11).

The metaphorical phrases for the onset and the cessa-
tion of God's wrath reveal something of the twofold use
of the terms for wrath. When it is a question of the
emotional disturbance, then the kindling or rising up
of the wrath, or the fact that Yahweh will assuage his
wrath, may have been used most frequently as in Ezek.
v.13, vi.12; Lam. iv.11; when it was a question of wrath
in action then the natural phrases are *raising wrath up*
as in II Chron. xxxvi.16; *sending it* in Job xx.23; Ps.
lxxviii.49; *carrying it out* in I Sam. xxviii.18; cf. Hos.
xi.9. One might be inclined to infer the same twofold
character from the differing use of the verb *return* (*šūb*)
for the ending of the wrath: Yahweh *ceases from his wrath*
in Exod. xxxii.12; II Kings xxiii.26; Jon. iii.9 (readily
linked with *repent*) or he *turns away his wrath* in Jer.
xviii.20; Ezra x.4; alternatively the *wrath is turned back*
in Jer. iv.6; Isa. v.25; Hos. xiv.4(5). But this last
phrase can also mean that the wrath has calmed down
(not only that its judgement has come to an end), so
that care must be exercised in making such distinctions

---

[1] Jer. [LXX, xxvii.25] has the literal rendering τὰ σκεύη ὀργῆς:
Isa. xiii.5—no doubt in view of verse 4 (ἔθνος ὁπλομάχον) has
οἱ ὁπλομάχοι (fighting with heavy weapons).
[2] Lam. iii.1 speaks of a *rod of wrath* (*'ebrāh*) as a metaphor for
wrath in action; cf. Job. ix.34, xxi.9 and Prov. xxii.8 (of human
wrath [*'ebrāh*]).

in view of the usage noted here. In the late period (of P and the Chronicler) the vaguer phrase *wrath comes* (*hāyāh*) is often used for the outbreak of the wrath (Num. i.53, xviii.5; Josh. xxii.20; I Chron. xxvii.24 *et passim*).

The basic effect of Yahweh's wrath is intended to be annihilation, complete obliteration. Thus it is said for instance in the exhortations of Deuteronomy: *the anger* (*'ap*) *of Yahweh would be kindled against you and he would speedily destroy you* (Deut. vii.4; cf. also ix.8, 19, 25 *et passim*) or in the Priestly writings: *I will consume them in a moment* in Num. xvi.21, xvii.10. The prophets too proclaim to Israel the all-consuming wrath of Yahweh (Ezek. xxii.31, xliii.8; Isa. xxx.28, xxxiv.2, 5, lxiii.1-3; Jer. l.13). Here we must notice that the prophets[1] describe the divine wrath not only in powerful metaphors, in part of cosmic proportions, and for this purpose bring into play the whole creation (Isa. xiii.13, xxx.30, xxxiv.2-4, lxvi.15 ff.; Ezek. xxxviii.22 *et passim*), but they bring it into relationship with actual historical events. Thus they interpret the affliction and the overthrow of their nation in past and present as the working of Yahweh's wrath which Israel comes to feel in separate onslaughts. Isaiah concludes his great poem of menaces with the refrain: *for all this his anger* (*'ap*) *is not turned away, and his hand is stretched out still* (ix.12 [Heb. 11], 17(16), 21(20); x.4, v.25).[2] According to him Yahweh hands over the people of his wrath to the Assyrian as the rod of his anger (x.5 f.; cf. ix.11(10) f.)[3]. For Israel the judgement of wrath consists above all in banishment from their land (*passim*). For the prophets,

---

[1] Just as in the Deuteronomic interpretation of history (see above).

[2] cf. Amos iv.6-12 (without the technical terms for wrath).

[3] With regard to other peoples too the nations become the weapons of his wrath (Isa. xiii.5; Jer. l.25) through whom he executes his judgement of wrath upon them, i.e. destroys them.

whether they look forwards or backwards, the exile is the chief example of God's wrath in action and in judgement. Similarly the early traditions, worked up and interpreted by the historians, record the destructive force and the terrifying dimensions of Yahweh's wrath, which achieves its purpose by drought and famine, pestilence and plague, wholesale slaughter of those affected, and abandonment to their enemies (Num. xi.1, 10, 33, xii.9, xvi.46 [Heb. xvii.11]; I Sam. vi.19; II Sam. xxiv *et passim*). With mysterious, irresistible power he falls upon them and lays low thousands[1] or strikes at individuals who presume to approach the Holy One (Exod. xix.1; II Sam. vi.7). It is of minor importance in this connection that at times the actual historical facts have perhaps not been reproduced in the same way as in the prophetic interpretation of history.

The proclamation of the prophets develops beyond the interpretation of events within history—perhaps in connection with earlier popular expectations[2]—more and more into the message of the final judgement of wrath in which Yahweh's claim to sovereignty prevails against all powers opposing him and brings history to an end. The prophets of the earlier period announce this judgement of wrath not only with regard to the 'nations', but also especially with regard to God's people which has turned away from its God.[3] In this sense they can speak of the Day of Yahweh, the 'day of wrath' as an eschatological event (Amos v.18-20; Isa. ii.6-21; Zeph. i.15, 18). From him no escape is

[1] In Num. xvi.49 (Heb. xvii.14), 14,700; in xxv.9, 24,000; in I Sam. vi.19, 50,070; in II Sam. xxiv.15, as many as 70,000 slain.

[2] cf. H. Gressmann, *Der Ursprung der israelitisch-jüdischen Eschatologie* (1905), pp. 144 f.

[3] It is not always possible to distinguish clearly in the prophetic writings (and elsewhere too in the OT) between the sway of the divine wrath within history or at the end of time; cf. therefore also p. 42.

possible for Israel—unless maybe that a few will be
hidden from him by means of a timely repentance
(Zeph. ii.1-3); nothing can avert the coming of the
judgement of wrath. It rests entirely with Yahweh's
love and merciful covenant to prevent wrath against
Israel spending itself to the full and through the judgement of wrath to bring about the time of salvation
which delivers Israel from the wrath. In the post-exilic
period, especially in later Judaism, the coming judgement of wrath is expected in the first place on the
nations (Ps. ix.17 f.; lvi.7[8]; lxxix.5-7[6-8]) and on the
wicked and ungodly within the congregation (Ps. vii.
6[7]; xi.5 f., xxviii.4, xciv.2), whilst the godly amongst
God's people believes that having experienced the forgiveness of his sins he is in safe keeping from the coming
wrath (Ps. xxx.6, lxv.3 f., ciii.3). It is true that at this
time too there can be no question of salvation being
certain, of relying firmly on escape from the approaching judgement of wrath, especially since the weight of
the wrath on the congregation and individuals amongst
it—in spite of all experience of the forgiveness of sins—
can never abolish the problem of the final appeasement
of the divine wrath (cf. p. 50).

It may befall the individual godly man—as can be
seen especially from the evidence of the later period[1]—to
experience some shortening of life and a threat to his
existence: sickness, oppression by personal enemies, the
menace of premature death and the consciousness that
God is far off, these are the signs of wrath (e.g. Ps.
lxxxviii.16, xc.7, 9, cii.8[9], 10 f.[11], 23 [24]). This is
displayed in a particularly impressive manner in the
book of Job. Here the righteous man feels that he has
been struck down by the wrath of God who has taken
from him not only possessions and health, but also his

[1] The individual acts of wrath mentioned above (e.g. II Sam.
vi.7) are here disregarded.

rights and his honour[1] and allows him in his wrath to discover the hidden nature of God (cf. below, pp. 37, 46).

iv. *The motives for divine wrath*

The search for the motives for divine wrath leads us to discuss God's inmost being and at the same time to fit the conception of his divine wrath into the presentation of God in the OT faith. A series of data in OT writings provides additional evidence that men saw themselves faced basically by an irrational and in the last resort inexplicable occurrence, befalling them with enigmatic and mysterious power.[2] Gen. xxxii.23-33 (Jacob's wrestling at the Jabbok) and Exod. iv.24 f. (Yahweh's attempt on Moses' life) betray an awareness of this. It is evident elsewhere too in various passages dealing with the sinister and fatal intervention of the holy God whom man may not see face to face (Exod. xxxiii.20; Judges xiii.22; Isa. vi.3), who destroys all that approaches his holiness too closely (Exod. xix.9-25, xx.18-21; Num. i.52 f.; I Sam. vi.19; II Sam. vi.7). In II Sam. xxiv.1 (Yahweh incites David to number the people), the motive for the unfounded and incomprehensible wrath of God is openly exposed (cf. also I Sam. xxvi.19=*if it is Yahweh who has stirred you up against me*). According to II Sam. xxi.14 Yahweh's wrath has been appeased; in xxiv.1 it breaks out again without any apparent reason; cf. also I Kings xxii.20 f. The change made in II Sam. xxiv by the Chronicler who replaces the wrath of Yahweh by Satan as the originator of David's temptation (I Chron. xxi.1), shows how vigorously later times repudiated such an interpretation. The lamentations of individuals in the

---

[1] cf. F. Baumgärtel, *Der Hiobdialog* (1933), p. 174.
[2] P. Volz, pp. 7-17.

Psalter and the book of Job in particular prove that the godly man was conscious of finding himself handed over to the wrath of Yahweh often for no reason. Thus the worshipper in Ps. lxxxviii, who has nothing to say about his guilt, complains to Yahweh whose *terrors I suffer from my youth up* that *thy wrath* (*hārōn*) *has swept over me* (verse 17), and Job rebels against God with the words: *He has torn me in his wrath* (*'ap*) *and hated me; he has gnashed his teeth at me* (xvi.9); *he has kindled* (*hārāh*) *his wrath* (*'ap*) *against me and counted me as his adversary* (xix.11). Admittedly this evidence from later times cannot be placed beside the early stories of sinister attack by divine wrath. The godly men of the post-exilic period measure their fate by the standard of strictly individual retribution which was not applied so consistently in earlier times. Nevertheless in the later as in the earlier period men were actively aware of being exposed to the behaviour of God which was so incomprehensible as to approximate to caprice and of which it may perhaps be more appropriate to say that the 'completely un-fathomable', 'the entirely other' is encountered, the *tremendum*.[1]

Here the element of Yahweh's inconceivable power and holiness outweighs other motives to be discussed later. But Yahweh's incomprehensible, terrifying be-haviour must not be explained as due to the absorbing of antiquity's faith in demons (cf. p. 25 n. 3), but it must be clearly stated that 'in the last resort "the demonic" in Yahweh has not been introduced into his nature, but is an original quality . . . is bound up with the inmost nature of this God and of his religion'.[2]

Yahweh's actions were indeed increasingly taken out of the sphere of the unaccountable and men were seeking more and more earnestly for an answer as to the

[1] Otto, pp. 21, 97. ET *The Idea of the Holy* (1928), pp. 19, 78; cf. Volz, p. 12 *et passim*. [2] Volz, p. 33.

4

cause of divine wrath.[1] It appears to be a reaction to man's behaviour or failure. With Israel in view it is felt to be the wrath of the God who has made known his will to save by pledges and guidance and who requires absolute devotion from the people, that is to say, worship of himself alone, complete trust and fulfilment of the demands imposed. It is the wrath of the God of the Covenant who has given the promises and the Law and has thereby bound Israel exclusively to himself.

Thus wrath, according to all the sources of the Pentateuch, strikes the people, or individual groups among them, when they revolt against Yahweh's saving will, when they murmur against his leadership during the desert wanderings (Num. xi.1(E), xvi.41-50 [Heb. xvii.6-15] (P), xiii.25-xiv.38(JE); Deut. i.34-36). When Achan broke faith (Josh. vii.1; xxii.20) and Saul spared Agag, king of the Amalekites, the wrath of Yahweh was kindled.[2] The open apostasy of the people from their God, the turning towards strange gods, is a particularly constantly recurring motive for divine anger against Israel.[3] From Exodus xxxii ('the golden calf') and Num. xxv (Ba'al Pe'or) it pervades not only the exhortations of Deuteronomy (xi.16 f., xii.23-xiii.19, xxix. 15-17; Josh. xxiii.16), but also the presentation of the history

---

[1] The first series of Job's speeches too are pervaded by the 'wherefore', searching for an explanation of the wrath (Job [iii.11], vii.20, x.18, xiii.24).

[2] The Priestly historical writing and exhortation presents the whole sphere of ritual and cult as overshadowed by God's wrath: Nadab and Abihu who wished to offer *strange* (?unholy) *fire* before the Lord are devoured by the fire of Yahweh's wrath (Lev. x.1 f.); wrong behaviour on the part of the priests may easily bring wrath upon the congregation (Lev. x.6); similarly it can be provoked by the profanation of the Sabbath (Neh. xiii.18).

[3] A. Ritschl has pointed out correctly that the real cause of God's anger is *defectus a foedere*, even though he has argued this in too one-sided a manner.

during the period of the judges and the kings with its essentially Deuteronomic interpretation.[1] We meet it also in the well-known sequence; apostasy of the people, this provokes Yahweh, wrath of Yahweh who sells Israel to foreign nations, etc.[2]

This reveals the mainsprings of the action of divine wrath with regard to Israel. We find them in their greatest breadth and depth in the prophets. These never weary of emphasising what Yahweh has done for Israel by choosing and guiding them[3] and against this background deliver their message of Yahweh's wrath.[4] Behind all the individual accusations of the prophets, whether they refer to the cult[5] or to social injustice,[6] to the policy of preparing for war and entering into alliances,[7] or simply to the worship of other gods,[8] there stands in the last resort the *one* great accusation: the nation has forgotten its God, has turned away from him and thereby despised his love.[9] This is the deepest root of the conception of wrath and this explains the whole overwhelming force of the message; it is Yahweh's wounded, holy love which arouses his wrath.[10] His wrath is analogous to his holiness (*qōdeš*) and to his

[1] Deut. iv. 25, ix.18; Judg. ii.14, iii.8, v.7; I Kings xiv.15, xvi. 33; II Kings xvii.17, xxi.6, xxii.17 *et passim*.

[2] The Chronicler gives similar motives in II Chron. xii.1-7, xvi.7-12, xxv.14-18 *et passim*.

[3] cf. e.g. Amos ii.9-11, iii.2; Hos.xi.1-6; Isa. i.2, v.1 f., xvii.10; Jer. ii.1-3, xxxi.1-3; Ezek. xvi.4-14.

[4] e.g. Hos. v.10, viii.5, xiii.11; Isa. ix.11; Jer. iv.4, xvii.4; Ezek. v.13, vii.3, xx.8, etc.

[5] Amos v. 21-27; Hos. vi.6; Isa. i.10-17; Jer. vi.20, vii.21-28.

[6] e.g. Amos v.7, 10-12; Isa. i.15-17; Mic. iii.1; Jer. v.28 *et passim*.

[7] cf. Hos. v.13, vii.11; Isa. xxx.1-5, xxxi.1-3; Jer. ii.35-37; Ezek. xvi.23 *et passim*.

[8] Alternatively what appears to be the worship of Yahweh in alien cultic forms.

[9] cf. above n. 3.   [10] Eichrodt, p. 125 (ET, p. 259).

mercy (*ḥesed*), Yahweh's care for Israel, which constitutes the foundation of the covenant relationship. The not infrequent association of the conception of Yahweh's jealousy (cf. TWNT II, pp. 880-882) with that of his anger throws light on this fact.[1]

The jealousy of Yahweh is rooted in the relationship between the holy God and his chosen people.[2] But election includes within it God's gracious condescension to Israel and his demand for the loyalty and obedience of his people. If Yahweh's love finds no response from his people and they turn to other gods, then Yahweh's 'jealousy' is kindled and this issues in wrath (Deut. xxxii.20 f.; cf. Ps. lxxviii.58, lxxxix.5) and brings about the rejection of Israel, his unfaithful wife (Ezek. xvi, xxiii). The same term 'jealousy', however, can denote Yahweh's concern for his people, as is attested from the exile onwards. Yahweh, as loving husband, stands in front of his people when they are threatened by other nations (Isa. xlii.13, lix.17, lxiii.15), and in his wrathful zeal brings destruction to the nations, but brings in salvation for his own (Zech. i.14 f., viii.2 f.; Nah. i.2).

Many parts of the message of God's wrath against the nations can be assigned to this motive. This is particularly evident in the post-exilic period when the intervention of the nations in Israel's life was experienced, as in the hatred of Edom and the intention of Babylon and other nations to destroy her;[3] in Israel Yahweh himself is attacked; his people's honour is his

---

[1] *Jealousy* (*qin'āh*) is found in association with the terms for wrath in: Deut. xxix.19; Ezek. xvi.38, xxxvi.6, and parallel with them in Deut. vi.15; Ezek. v.13, xvi.42; Zeph. iii.8; Ps. lxxxix.5; Nah. i.2.

[2] cf. F. Küchler, 'Der Gedanke des Eifers Jahves im AT', ZAW 28 (1908), pp. 42-52.

[3] Jer. x.25 (late): *Pour out thy wrath upon the nations that knew thee not . . . for they have devoured Jacob*; cf. Zech. ii. 1-4; Mal. i.3 f. *et passim*.

own honour (Isa. xlviii.9-11 and especially Ezekiel). Here a genuine concern of the prophets is expressed, though at times in the post-exilic period it is formulated in too exaggerated and one-sided a manner. The same motive already dominates the earlier historical writings when it is a matter of describing how Yahweh enforces his saving will against the enemies of his people (Exod. xviii.27-30; Josh. xxiv.12; Num. xxiv.18).[1] The basic foundation of this motive for Yahweh's wrath against the nations is his absolute claim to rule the whole world, a claim directed against the *hubris* of the nations (cf. Gen. xi) and their rulers, against their tyranny, and also against the infringement of his universally valid commandments. Thus Isaiah announces Yahweh's judgement to the Assyrian, called to be the rod of his anger against Israel, because he has over-stepped the limits of his authority (Isa. x.5-15; cf. xiv.4-6, xvi.6; Ezek. xxv.15-17, xxviii.1-17; Zech. i.15). In the same way his wrath strikes (Deut. xxix.23 [Heb. 22]) the immoral doings of Sodom and Gomorrah (Gen. xix), the Moabites' lack of awe (Amos ii.1) and the wickedness of Nineveh (Jonah i.2).[2]

Beyond all this we find that the OT proclaims the divine wrath in action throughout all human life. It interprets troubles and the finiteness of life as the result of the *hubris* of men and the guilt in which this involves them. From the fall of the first man (Gen. ii-iii) this train of thought leads through the increasing wickedness of men (Gen. vi-viii) and their plans to reach the heavens (Gen. xi) to the final verdict of the psalmist: *For we are consumed by thy anger ('ap); and by thy wrath (ḥēmāh) we are overwhelmed* in Ps. xc.7, which points to human sin to justify it (cf. verse 8); cf. also Job xiv.1-4:

---

[1] cf. Ritschl, *Rechtfertigung und Versöhnung* II, p. 128.

[2] The ethical motive by itself for Yahweh's wrath against the nations appears comparatively seldom in the OT.

Man that is born of a woman is of few days and full of trouble . . . who can bring a clean thing out of an unclean?[1] According to this all human life is a life of sin and is subject to the ever active wrath of God.

v. *The onset, duration and averting of divine wrath*

When examining the onset of the wrath, its duration and averting, we must again make a distinction between its action within history and at the end of time. In this section we are considering chiefly historical wrath (for wrath as an eschatological occurrence cf. p. 34). Yahweh's wrath against Israel is carried into effect within the history of his people by individual acts and in particular by the exile of the nation. In this sense the 'day of wrath' which is expected or has already arrived can be spoken of as an event within history (cf. TWNT II, p. 947), in fact by remembering the fate of the nation (Ezek. vii.19, xxii.24; Lam. i.12, 21, ii.1, 21 f.), and also that of the individual (Job xx.28, xxi.30; Prov. xi.4). Not infrequently, especially in the historical writings of the OT, the onset of the divine wrath is described as a sudden blow, as breaking in unheralded. Like lightning it strikes those who have sinned against Yahweh (Exod. xix.12; Num. xi.33, xii.9, xvii.6-11, xxv.9-11; II Sam. vi.7).

On the other hand the OT testifies many times to Yahweh's forbearance (cf. TWNT IV, pp. 378-381), so that he does not allow his wrath free play, but restrains it and waits patiently (Exod. xxxiv.6 f.; Num. xiv.18; Nah. i.3; Isa. xlviii.9; Ps. ciii.8). By means of individual blows he warns Israel and exhorts them to repent before he proceeds in his wrath to complete annihilation. The prophetic writings contain proof of

[1] G. Hölscher, *Das Buch Hiob* (Handbuch zum AT I, 17, 1937) *ad loc.* deletes the last words on the ground of rhythm ('metrically unsatisfactory'), but this is scarcely correct; cf. Job iv.17. [But cf. F. Horst, *Hiob* (1960 ff.), p. 207.]

this in many places, both in utterances of wrath (e.g. Amos. iv.6-11; Isa. ix.12 [Heb. 11] and parallels; Jer. iv.4), and also in the passages quoted above making a loving appeal (cf. p. 39 n. 3). When turning to Israel in his mercy,[1] Yahweh either prevents his wrath from taking effect (cf. especially Hos. xi.9)[2] or he shows kindness to his people.[3] By his forbearance he gives Israel an opportunity for penitence and repentance. This applies also to his forbearance towards Nineveh of which Jonah complained; whilst elsewhere in the case of the enemies of his people Yahweh's patient waiting (Jer.xv.15; Ps. vii.6 [Heb. 7], lxxvii.9 [Heb. 10] *et passim*) is due to the wish on the one hand to test and to chastise his people and on the other to bring more clearly into the open the guilt of their enemies.

Those who groan under the effects of the wrath as it is expressed in the course of history repeatedly ask how long it will endure. Jeremiah already puts the question into the people's mouth: *Will he be angry for ever, will he be indignant to the end?* (iii.5) and declares Yahweh's reply: *Return . . . for I am merciful. . . . I will not be angry for ever* (iii.12).[4] During the exile the hope is born that Yahweh's anger with his people has come to an end (Isa. xl.2; cf. Ps. ciii.9); in Deutero-Isaiah it is founded on the well-known passage: *In overflowing wrath for a moment I hid my face from you, but with perpetual mercy* (*ḥesed*)[5] *I will have compassion on you. . . . I have sworn that*

[1] Yahweh's forbearance is based on mercy (*ḥesed*) and compassion (*raḥᵃmîm*) (cf. TWNT II, pp. 475-479).

[2] *I will not execute my fierce anger . . . for I am God and not man, the Holy One in your midst and I will not come to destroy.*

[3] cf. Exod. xxxiv.6 f.; Num. xiv.18; Nah. i.3 (*and will by no means clear the guilty*).

[4] These verses do not belong to the same context, but their content may be brought together.

[5] The Isaiah scroll reads the plural, cf. *The Dead Sea Scrolls of St. Mark's Monastery* I (1950), Pl. 45.

I will not be angry with you (liv.8-10). And yet particularly after the exile the question of the duration of the
wrath is heard again and again in the psalms (Ps.
lxxix.5, lxxxv.5 [Heb. 6], lxxxix.46 [Heb. 47]) and in
the words of the prophets (Hag. i.5-11; Zech. i.3, 12).
To a greater extent than before the exile the congregation is aware from its life—just as the individual is
aware of it in his own lot—of the burden of God's
wrath. It is this experience which later produces in the
apocalyptic writings the recognition that the 'period of
wrath' prevails and must run its course, before the time
of mercy can dawn (Isa. xxvi.20; Dan. viii.19, xi.36;
cf. p. 17). This, it is hoped, will bring the wrath to an
end. On the other hand with regard to Yahweh's
enemies apart from Israel it can be proclaimed that his
wrath lasts for ever (cf. Nah. i.2), and in Mal. i.4 Edom
is described as *the people with whom Yahweh is angry for ever*.
Here the reflections on wrath within history and in the
eschatological sphere overlap. At the same time the
fact is expressed that Yahweh's wrath against the
nations is the reverse side of his care for Israel: the
enemies of Yahweh (and of the people) who thwart his
saving will, are destined for complete destruction.

The law was given with the purpose of warding off
Yahweh's devouring wrath and of preserving for Israel
the favour and mercy of its God, and this was largely
the aim too of the prophetic preaching,[1] for Yahweh is
a jealous God who punishes sins. Thus a warning in
the framework of Deuteronomy ends with the words
*lest the anger of Yahweh your God be kindled against you and he
destroy you from off the face of the earth* (Deut. vi.15). The
later period assigns to the cult and its servants the
crucial role of preserving the congregation from the

[1] The proclamation of inescapable judgement includes again
and again the call to repentance and penitence which alone gives
hope of preservation from the judgement of wrath.

threat of the divine wrath. The Levites are to encamp round the tent of the testimony *that there may be no wrath upon the congregation of the people Israel* (Num. i.53).[1]

Yet the people struck by God's wrath are denied the means of averting it, known and practised by Israel's neighbours, namely magical procedures for exorcising the deity.[2] On the contrary it was always evident that in the last resort Yahweh would avert his wrath of his own free will, and this would be an act of mercy and loving-kindness.[3] It is to Yahweh's mercy that the prayer to avert or curb his wrath is directed.[4] This has already appeared in the question about the duration of the wrath (cf. p. 43) and indications of it can be detected again and again elsewhere too,[5] for instance in the Deuteronomic formula.[6] Intercession for those threatened or struck by the wrath appeals to God's mercy. Thus Moses prays for the people in their backsliding (Exod. xxxii.11 f., 31 f.; Num. xi.1 f., xiv.11-13; Deut. ix.19; Ps. cvi.23) or for individuals who have become guilty (Num. xii.13; Deut. ix.20); Amos for Israel (vii.2, 5); Jeremiah for Judah (xiv.7-9, xviii.20); Job for his friends (xlii.7 f.). Such intercession is accepted by Yahweh and the effects of the wrath are

---

[1] This precaution surely does not merely express the fact that the sphere of the cult and the ritual is particularly exposed to God's wrath (Cr.-Kö. 812).

[2] Eichrodt, p. 126 (ET p. 261); M. Jastrow, *Die Religion Babyloniens and Assyriens* I (1905), ch. 16; cf. S. H. Hooke, *Babylonian and Assyrian Religion* (1953, 1962), pp. 71-79; Num. xvi.41-50 [Heb. xvii.6-15] describes a plan for expiation ordered by Moses.

[3] This does not mean that Yahweh does not demand punishment and expiation for the guilt incurred.

[4] cf. F. Heiler, *Das Gebet*[2] (1920), p. 87; ET *Prayer* (1932), p. 33.

[5] '*When the people cried to Yahweh, Yahweh raised up a deliverer for the people* in Judg. iii.9 *et passim* (cf. p. 39).

[6] cf. also the plea to restrain the wrath in Isa. lxiv.9 [Heb. 8]; Jer. x.24; Ps. vi.1 [Heb. 2]; xxxviii.2 and Yahweh's consent in Jer. xxx.11.

reduced (Num. xiv; Deut. ix) or averted altogether
(Num. xi; II Sam. xxiv). But the time may come when
Yahweh no longer yields to intercession (Amos vii.8,
viii.2; Ezek. xiv.14), and indeed forbids his servant
outright to offer it (Jer. vii.16). Then nothing can
avert the wrath any longer and it comes into action
irresistibly, overpoweringly (Ezek. viii.18, xiv.14). The
decisive motive for the intercession, the reference to
Yahweh's connection with Israel (Exod. xxxii.12; Num.
xiv.15 f.; Ps. lxxiv.2), his mercy and faithfulness to the
covenant (Num. xiv.18; cf. Deut. xiii.18), is occasionally supplemented by emphasising the weakness and
creatureliness of the object of his wrath. Thus Amos
substantiates his plea for Israel with the words: *How
should Jacob stand for he is small* in vii.2, 5 and the
Psalmist: *for we are brought very low* in lxxix.8.[1]

The book of Job brings out particularly clearly the
human creatureliness and the inability of man to with-
stand the onward rush of God's wrath. Admittedly
Job's speeches in the discourses testify rather to the fact
that man has succcumbed inescapably to God's wrath
and does not know about his love, with its readiness to
forgive, and could only come to feel the force of his
terrible power, so that in his defencelessness he begs that
God may let him off (Job vii.1-20, 21, ix.18-22, xiii.13-
22, xiv, especially verses 1-6). At the same time in view
of the present arrangement of the book of Job, it must be
observed that the reader is clearly told to start with that
Job's puzzling fate is not the consequence of the blind
fury of divine anger, but that his grievous lot has a
particular cause.[2]

[1] cf. also the reasons given for Yahweh's ceasing from wrath in Isa.
lvii.16; Ps. lxxviii.39; also F. Hesse, *Die Fürbitte im AT* (Diss.
Erlangen, 1950).
[2] J. Fichtner, 'Hiob in der Verkündigung unserer Zeit', in
Jahrbuch der Theologischen Schule Bethel (1950), pp. 71 ff., 88.

Since Yahweh's wrath is a manifestation of his holiness which has been violated by apostasy from the covenant and by infringement of his ordinances, he can combine his turning away from wrath and his gracious turning towards his people with punishment and reconciliation. Thus his wrath departed from Israel after their desertion to Ba'al Pe'or when the guilty had been slain (Num. xxv.1-5 (JE)), i.e. after Phinehas had given an example and pierced the wrongdoers caught in the act (Num. xxv.6-11 (P)).[1] The same thing happened after the extermination of Achan and his family who had stolen devoted objects (Josh. vii.1, 25 f., cf. II Sam. xxi.4). The OT speaks comparatively seldom of divine wrath being averted by propitiatory offerings (Num. xvii.11; II Sam. xxiv(17 ff.); Ps. lxxviii.38 and probably also I Sam. xxvi.19; cf. TWNT III, pp. 302-311). The prophets announce that Yahweh's wrath may perhaps still be averted by turning away from evil ways, by repentance and penitence (Jer. iv.4, 8, xxxvi.7; cf. Dan. ix.16 *et passim*), and Deutero-Isaiah promises the people in exile the end of divine wrath after it has expiated its guilt: *drunk to the dregs the cup of his wrath* (li.17, 22) and *received double for all her sins* (xl.2).

vi. *The relationship of divine wrath to God's holiness, his righteousness and his mercy*

Once only in the OT is the wrath of God singled out particularly as a feature of God's nature; this occurs in the context of God's wrath against his enemies, not against his own people in Nah. i.2: *avenging and wrathful.*[2]

---

[1] Phinehas by his action confirmed Yahweh's zeal for Israel (Num. xxv.11).

[2] *Jealous God* (*qannā*) (5 times in Exodus and Deuteronomy) and *qannō'* (twice) occurs more frequently. The phrase in Ps. vii.12 is not sufficiently well attested textually (cf. LXX).

This fact must not deceive us into supposing that the
proclamation of God's wrath is not inextricably bound
up with the whole message of the OT. God's wrath is
the power of the holy God who asserts and enforces his
absolute claim to rule. Even though—so far as the
actual terminology is concerned—God's holiness is seldom associated with his wrath (cf. Ps. lxxviii.38-41),[1]
yet in fact this association is incontestable. This is
already demonstrated by God's wrath being again
and again described in phrases and similes associated
with those used for a theophany (cf. Ps. xviii; Exod.
xix; Isa. xxx; Hab. iii). Thus divine wrath is conceived
and described not as the consequence of an objective
power controlled by fate, but of a subjective will controlled by a person. It describes an 'emotional disturbance' of God[2] and its expression by an attack on all the
powers which oppose God's holy will. This formula
covers completely Yahweh's wrath against Israel and
the nations, against individuals and against mankind.
With regard to God's people there is indeed a particularly deep-seated reason for Yahweh's wrath since
by its means Yahweh's holy love and his reaction to the
ingratitude and unfaithfulness of Israel in the face of his
care for them is made known.[3]

Yet at the same time Yahweh's wrath is not simply
identical with his righteousness as a judge. On the
contrary it is significant that Yahweh's righteousness is
never explicitly connected with his wrath, although in
numberless passages the reasons adduced for the operations of the divine wrath are the commissions and

[1] Cr.-Kö. p. 810; in Hos. xi.9 Yahweh's holiness is contrasted
with his wrath.   [2] Weber, p. 11.
[3] If this can in the last resort be considered as the common
denominator for God's wrath, yet we must not forget how varied
are its representations in detail at different times and by different
OT witnesses.

omissions of Israel (or of mankind), which affront God's sovereign claim and his concrete demands.[1] Job actually turns from the God who is angry with him and hostile to him to the God who as his advocate should procure him his rights, i.e. to the God of righteousness[2] (Job xvi.20 f.). These facts prove clearly that the men of the OT felt the divine wrath to be irrational, incalculable, subjectively wilful, whilst they themselves, having regard to God's righteousness see themselves directed rather to his revealed will. No doubt Yahweh's wrath has its reason and its occasion, but its effects, its duration and the escape from it cannot be foreseen, much less calculated or measured. Of course the reason and the occasion for God being angry may also remain completely in the dark and concealed;[3] thus so far as man can see, for example in the discourses in Job and in individual psalms, wrath and injustice approach each other. Perhaps this enables us to understand the request which we read occasionally (Jer. x.24; Ps. vi.1 [Heb. 2]; xxxviii.1 [Heb. 2]) that Yahweh may chasten 'in just measure', so to speak according to his justice and not in his overflowing wrath; hence the anxiety lest wrath should gain the ascendency in God's being, as suggested in the question of the Psalmist: *Has God forgotten to be gracious? Has he in anger shut up his compassion?* (Ps. lxxxvii.9 [Heb. 10]).[4] Yet it is hardly possible to use such passages and similar ones as the basis for the assertion that 'it is typical of the OT view of God that

[1] Eichrodt, p. 129 (ET, p. 266).

[2] cf. J. Hempel's remark: 'At the moment when God is under the sway of anger, it is needful that he should direct his thoughts to his true self' ('Das Problem des Hiob', ZSTh 7 (1929), p. 675, n. 2) is justified only with the meaning given by Job who does not know the occasion for his grievous lot and attributes it to the unwarrantable wrath of God.

[3] Or must first be discovered (e.g. Josh. vii).

[4] cf. Hab. iii.2: *In wrath remember mercy.*

love and wrath lie side by side in the divine nature, just as they do in an oriental ruler, without being harmonised in any way'.[1] On the contrary Yahweh's wrath with regard to Israel is the reverse side of his love for them; closely bound up with it is the conception of his jealousy (cf. p. 40). And when Deutero-Isaiah allows us to catch a glimpse of the struggle between wrath and compassion in God's heart, we do not look into the heart of a tyrant who dispenses wrath and love at random, but we see how mercy and compassion can restrain the overflowing wrath of Yahweh and how finally compassion retains the victory (Isa. liv.8-10; cf. Jer. xxxi.20). Thus the worshipper in Psalm xxx can confess: *his anger is but for a moment, and his favour is for a life-time* (verse 5 [Heb. 6])[2] and the song of praise in Isaiah xii can thank him for turning away his wrath. Beside these avowals of divine compassion there stand, it is true—especially in the earlier period—the declarations of an inescapable judgement of wrath on the people of God, and in the later times too, which expect God's wrath to fall mainly on the nations and the ungodly, there is even for the congregation no certainty that they will be saved from the approaching wrath which has overtaken all evil-doers (e.g. Jer. xxx.24; Isa. xiii.11).

[1] J. Lindblom, 'Zur Frage der Eigenart der alttestamentlichen Religion', BZAW 66 (1963), p. 135.

[2] Unless *stroke* (*nega'*) should be read for *moment* (*rega'*) with Halévy (thus H. Gunkel, *Psalmen* ([4]1926), p. 126); i.e. *his anger is a blow, his favour is life.*

III. GOD'S WRATH IN THE SEPTUAGINT

1. *The linguistic usage of the Septuagint*

i. ὀργή and θυμός

THE LXX uses primarily ὀργή and θυμός[1] for rendering the various Hebrew expressions denoting 'wrath' (pp. 14 ff.). By their etymology and the range of their meanings these two terms are clearly distinguished from each other. The difference between them is that ' θυμός denotes the emotion, ὀργή its outward appearance and expression. . . . θυμός is wrath rising up within, ὀργή wrath breaking out'.[2] But in the linguistic usage of the LXX the difference between ὀργή and θυμός is completely obliterated. This will be proved by the following survey of the use of ὀργή and θυμός and the verbs associated with them. In doing so it is not necessary to distinguish on principle whether the terms denote the wrath of God or of men. This will be indicated explicitly only in special cases.

(a) ὀργή and θυμός are found associated with each other; in Deut. ix.19 Moses refers to God's wrath against Israel as ὀργή ('ap) and θυμός (ḥēmāh); Ps. lxxviii [LXX, lxxvii], 49 places θυμός ('ebrāh), ὀργή (zaʿam) and θλῖψις (ṣārāh) side by side; cf. also Ps. cii [LXX, ci], 10 [Heb. 11] Mic. v.15 [Heb. 14]; Isa. xiii.9; Jer. vii.20; Ezek. v.13 *et passim*.

(b) In the *parallelismus membrorum* both terms appear alternately in accordance with the laws of Hebrew poetry: so in Hos. xiv.11; Isa. xxxiv.2; cf. also Ezek.

---

[1] The ὀργή of God is mentioned well over 200 times, that of man about 50 times; the θυμός of God just 200 times, that of men 70 times. It is most noteworthy that in the LXX θυμός is used so frequently, and as a synonym for ὀργή, for God's wrath, whilst in secular Greek it never designates divine wrath (cf. Irmscher, pp. 3ff.).   [2] Cr.-Kö. 807; cf. p. 1.

vii.5; xxii.31, Ps. ii.5; vi.1 (Heb. 2), xxxviii (LXX, xxxvii), 1 (Heb. 2), xc (LXX, lxxxix), 11; Prov. xv.1, xxvii.4 *et passim*. The corresponding adjectives and verbs also appear in parallel members of a verse, as, e.g. in Prov. xxii.24.

(c) The two words connected by the genitive θυμὸς τῆς ὀργῆς (or θυμός ὀργῆς) and ὀργὴ τοῦ θυμοῦ (or ὀργὴ θυμοῦ) are used in exactly the same sense and both usually render *ḥᵃrōn 'ap* : Exod. xxxii.12; Num. xxxii.14; Jer. iv.26; Ps. lxix (LXX, lxviii), 24 (Heb. 25) *et passim*; occasionally they stand for a single Hebrew term: in Job iii.17, xxxvii.2; Ezek. xxxiii.25; Ps. cvi (LXX, cv), 23 (Codex Vaticanus); Isa. ix.18, xiii.13.

(d) The combination θυμοῦσθαι ὀργῇ (Gen. xxxix.19; Josh. vii.1; Isa. v.25) is frequently found; less often ὀργὴ θυμοῦται (I Sam. xi.6; II Kings xxiii.26). The latter is always, the former is almost without exception, the translation of *ḥārāh 'ap*. The construction θυμοῦσθαι θυμῷ or θυμόν does not occur in the LXX according to Hatch and Redpath.[1] More frequent than θυμοῦσθαι ὀργῇ is the phrase ὀργίζεσθαι θυμῷ (e.g. in Exod. xvii.24; Deut. vii.4; Judges ii.14; Ps. cvi [LXX, cv], 40). Like the very rare θυμὸς ὀργίζεται (Judges vi.39; Ps. lxxiv [LXX, lxxiii], 1; cxxiv [LXX, cxxiii], 3) it is almost always a rendering of *ḥārāh 'ap*. The construction ὀργίζεσθαι ὀργήν in Zech. i.2, 15 corresponds to *qāṣap qeṣep* in the Masoretic text; in the form ὀργίζεσθαι ὀργῇ it occurs in II Chron. xxix.8 for *hāyāh qeṣep*.

(e) The number of phrases formed with ὀργή or with θυμός to reproduce the Hebrew original is astonishingly great. We are only offering a selection of them and as far as possible are giving equal consideration to both terms in our references to the passages.[2] The following

[1] *Concordance to the Septuagint* (1897-1906).

[2] The first passage in each case attests ὀργή (or ὀργὴ θυμοῦ) the second θυμός (or θυμὸς ὀργῆς).

verbs can be used with ὀργή and θυμός as the subject:
ἀναβαίνειν (Ps. lxxviii [LXX, lxxvii], 21; Ezek. xxiv.8);
γίνεσθαι (Josh. xxii.20; Lam. iii.47); εἶναι (II Chron.
xix.10; Lev. x.6); ἔρχεσθαι (Job iii.26, xxxvi.18 [Codex
Alexandrinus]);[1] ἐκκαίεσθαι (Deut. xxix.20 [Heb. 19];
Jer. xliv [LXX, li], 6); παύεσθαι (Job xiv.13; Isa. i.24);
ἀποστρέφειν (intransitive. Hos. xiv.5; Jer. xxiii.20);
ἀποστρέφεσθαι (Num. xxv.4; Dan. ix.16); ἐνχεῖσθαι (II
Kings xxii.13; Jer. vii.20 [Codex Alexandrinus]) and
others. ὀργή and θυμός are found in the accusative of the
object and governed by ἐγείρειν (Prov. xv.1; Ecclus.
xxxvi.7); ἐκκαίειν (Ps. lxxviii [LXX, lxxvii], 38); Job
iii.17 [Codex Vaticanus differs]); ἐξαποστέλλειν (Ps.
lxxviii [LXX, lxxvii], 49a and b); ἀποστρέφειν (Prov.
xxix.8; Ps. lxxviii [LXX, lxxvii], 38); συντελεῖν (Ezek.
v.13; Lam. iv.11); ἐκχεῖν (Zeph. iii.8; Ezek. ix.8).
Other phrases with ὀργή or θυμός as the object are rare.
Both are found depending on the adjective πλήρης in Isa.
xxx.27; Wisd. v.22[2]; they are also used as attributes to
the noun ἡμέρα (Job xx.28; Zeph. ii.2)[3]; καιρός (Ecclus.
xliv.17; Jer. xviii.23); πῦρ (Ezek. xxi.31, xxxvi.5);
πλῆθος (Ps. ix.25; Isa. xxxi.4) and ῥάβδος (Isa. x.5).

In contrast to this considerable quantity of phrases
which can be formed equally well with ὀργή or θυμός,
there is a substantially smaller number of constructions
attested with ὀργή alone and not with θυμός, and vice
versa. None of these cases taken either singly or as a
whole, provides a criterion for distinguishing the concepts of ὀργή and θυμός. So they are not adduced here
in extenso.[4] It is striking how often ὀργή and θυμός are

[1] Compounds of ἔρχεσθαι are also found.
[2] Both are also found with the same prepositions.
[3] ἡμέρα θυμοῦ occurs only in Zeph. ii.2 and Prov. xi.4 (LXX,
Vaticanus and Sinaiticus omit); elsewhere always, including other
passages in Zephaniah, ἡμέρα ὀργῆς· is found.
[4] Most of the phrases in question are used once only.

5

interchanged in the manuscripts of the LXX.[1] If there were a distinction between the two concepts, based on their meaning, or even only on their usage, these frequent interchanges would hardly have been possible. All this goes to show that ὀργή and θυμός, as well as the verbs associated with them, can be used completely indifferently, and are in fact so used in the LXX.

ii. ὀργίζω (θυμόω), παροργίζω, παροργισμός

Active forms of ὀργίζω and θυμόω, both meaning *to make angry, to provoke to wrath* (trans.) are each attested reliably only once (Job xii.6 [Alexandrinus]; Hos. xii.14 [Heb. 15]). On the other hand the passive form of ὀργίζω is found in nearly 80 passages, that of θυλόω in more than 60, often emphasised by θυμῷ or by ὀργῇ (cf. p. 52), always with the meaning *to grow angry, to be wroth*. Either God or man can be the subject of ὀργίζομαι and θυμόομαι. Similarly the active παροργίζω,[2] used in more than 50 passages, has the transitive meaning of *making angry, provoking to wrath*. It is surprising how seldom the LXX uses the two associated nouns παροργισμός (6 times) and παρόργισμα, not found in the NT, (3 times). They mean *provocation, cause of anger* (I Kings xv.30; II Chron. xxxv.19c [not in Hebrew text]), and also in the wider sense denote an action provoking wrath (LXX, II Esdras xix.18 [=Hebrew Neh. ix.18]; I Kings xvi.33). The subject of παροργίζειν is man (except in Deut. xxxii.21).[3] παροργισμός and παρόργισμα too when in the active mood are only used of man. In two passages παροργισμός is used with a passive meaning: II Kings xiv.3 and Jer. xxi.5.

---

[1] cf. Isa. x.4; Jer. x.25; Lam. iv.11; II Chron. xxix.8 *et passim*.

[2] Not in the active only in Dan. xi.36 and Ecclus. iv.2.

[3] Here the occasion is the contrast with Israel's provocation.

iii. ὀργίλος *and* θυμώδης

ὀργίλος occurs as an adjective 4 times (Ps. xviii [LXX, xvii], 49 and 3 times in Proverbs), as an adverb once (IV Macc. viii.9); θυμώδης is found 8 times (5 times in Proverbs, twice in Ecclus., once in Jer xxx [LXX, xxxvii], 23). Thus both are used predominantly in the Wisdom literature. They mean *inclined to anger, passionate*, and apart from Jer. xxx [LXX, xxxvii], 23, denote only a human quality.

iv. (κότος), χόλος, *and* μῆνις

These three terms which are used in secular Greek only to signify divine wrath,[1] are in the LXX not employed for the wrath of God. κότος is not found at all, χόλος in 5 passages only (Prov. xvi.28 [Sinaiticus]; Eccles. v.16; II Macc. iii [Alexandrinus], 28; III Macc. v.1, 30) and the verb (ἐκ) χολᾶν only in III Macc. iii.1. In all 6 passages the wrath of man is meant.[2] Μῆνις occurs 4 times (Gen. xlix.7; Num. xxxv.21; Ecclus. xxvii.30, xxviii.5); μηνίαμα or μήνιμα[3] only in Ecclus. xl.5; the associated verb μηνίειν 5 times (Lev. xix.18; Jer. iii.12; Ps. ciii [LXX, cii], 9; Ecclus. x.6, xxviii.7). In 8 of these 10 passages human wrath is meant; only in Jer. iii.12 and Ps. ciii.9 is the verb connected with God and in both cases it must be noted that an irreconcilable μηνίειν by God is explicitly denied. All these facts lead to the conclusion that the Greek translators considered κότος, χόλος and μῆνις and their derivatives were too definitely tainted by their use as the expressions for the wrath of the (Greek) gods and

---

[1] In secular Greek they are used almost exclusively in poetic language (Kleinknecht).

[2] In Eccles. v.16 it stands for *qeṣep*, in Prov. xvi.28 there is no Hebrew counterpart; the other passages are in II and III Macc.

[3] The LXX has μήνιμα (Sinaiticus and Alexandrinus) or μηνίαμα (Vaticanus).

were not suitable technically; in consequence they avoided them intentionally when it was a matter of indicating the wrath of the God of the Scriptures.

2. *Interpretations given in the Septuagint*

On the whole the LXX translators have reproduced correctly the original Hebrew in the OT passages dealing with wrath. It must be admitted that in so doing they worked at times somewhat mechanically; for instance they rendered *ḥēmāh*, one of the chief Hebrew terms for wrath[1] by θυμός even in those passages where it means the *poison* of snakes or of arrows (Deut. xxxii.24; Ps. lviii.4 [Heb. 5]; Job vi.4); only in Ps. cxl [LXX, cxxxix], 3 (Heb. 4) do we read ἰός which we should expect. *Kaʿas (kaʿaś)* found 25 times in the OT and usually meaning *annoyance, resentment, trouble*, is rendered in the LXX almost exclusively by ὀργή (9 times),[2] θυμός (8 times), παροργισμός (twice) and παρόργισμα (once), thus with typical terms for wrath; only quite seldom do other translations appear: I Sam. i.16 (Alexandrinus), ἀθυμία; Prov. xxi.19 γλωσσώδης (beside ὀργίλος) and in Eccles. i.18 probably γνῶσις. *Rūaḥ* is translated in some passages with ὀργή (Prov. xvi.32) or θυμός (Zech. vi.8; Prov. xxix.11), in others, where this rendering would be at least equally obvious, with πνεῦμα (Judges viii.3; Isa. xxv.4, xxx. 28); *mērūah ʾappō* (*at the blast of his anger*) in Job iv.9 with ἀπὸ πνεύματος ὀργῆς. The LXX has several times replaced the concrete means or effects of God's wrath in action by the abstract word *wrath*, thus in Jer. xxx [LXX, xxxvii], 23 *storm of God* is replaced by ὀργή; similarly—and perhaps more strikingly because the context here does not deal with God's wrath—in Ps. lxxxiii [LXX, lxxxii], 16.

[1] When meaning *wrath* it is rendered 70 times by θυμός and 25 times by ὀργή.

[2] In addition once by ὀργίλος.

The translation of '*ap* in two cases, where it does not
mean *wrath*, but *nose*, is particularly characteristic.
When it is a question of a man's nose (Prov. xxx.33) or
the snout of an animal (Prov. xi.22), the LXX can say
μυκτήρ or ῥίς; it is said of idols too (Ps. cxv.6 [LXX,
cxiii.14]).[1] On the other hand the phrase in Ps. xviii
(LXX, xvii), 8 (Heb. 9) evidently aroused the translators' scruples; so they rendered it with ἀνέβη καπνὸς ἐν
ὀργῇ αὐτοῦ. Similarly they translate verse 15 (Heb.
16): *at the blast of the breath of thy nostrils* with ἀπὸ ἐμπ-
νεύσεως πνεύματος ὀργῆς αὐτοῦ. Clearly they can endure
more easily the anthropopathic phrase about God's
wrath than the anthropomorphic one about God's nose
given in the Hebrew text. In other passages the Greek
aversion to the passions (πάθη) suggests to the LXX
translators the replacement of the conception of God's
wrath by other concepts. Thus several times instead of
speaking of God's wrath, they have mentioned human
sin which provoked it. Cf. Job xlii.7; Num. i.53;
similarly Isa. lvii.17; I Esdras vi.14 (15) [cf. Ezra
v.12] (TWNT I, p. 289).[2] Mal. i.4 also contains a
change in the interpretation. The apocalyptic punishment is not said to be as stated in the Masoretic text:
the people with whom the Lord is angry for ever, but the LXX
has substituted for it: *the people against whom the Lord
stands prepared for battle so long as the world endures*. In Isa.
lxvi.14 the Masoretic text reads: *and his* (Yahweh's)
indignation against his enemies. The LXX has altered both
conceptions and has thereby made allowance for the
more ethical and rational idea of God in Hellenism.
Perhaps the greatest change is in Zech. i.12: κύριε

---

[1] In Amos iv.10 the words *the stench of your camp into your nostrils*,
obviously the result of a misreading, are understood quite differently in the LXX.

[2] cf. Weber p. 155 for such changes of interpretation in the
Targum as well.

παντόκρατωρ, ἕως τίνος οὐ μὴ ἐλεήσῃς τὴν Ἰερουσαλημ καὶ τὰς πόλεις Ἰουδα, ἃς ὑπερεῖδες (Heb. *zā'am have indignation*) τοῦτο ἐβδομηκοντὸν ἔτος; here undoubtedly national pride is playing a role in addition to the changed conception of God. In Hab. iii the whole chapter is involved. In the Masoretic text it is a psalm about the manifestation of the wrathful God. In the LXX this recedes behind the revelation through his word. By what appears to be a double translation in verse 2 (cf. BH³) this statement is produced: *when my soul is confused by* (God's) *wrath then thou wilt remember thy mercy*. Thereby the remark interjected into the Masoretic text, which is perhaps after all only a gloss, becomes a principal sentence. In verse 5 the terrible weapon of pestilence (*deber*) is replaced by revelation through the λόγος (*dābār*). Whilst in the Masoretic text Yahweh is the subject throughout the whole chapter, in the LXX λόγος becomes the key-word in verses 5-9. Not until later are the statements about it put into God's mouth by the λέγει κύριος in verse 9. Again in verse 12 we read: ἐν ἀπειλῇ ὀλιγώσεις γῆν καὶ ἐν θυμῷ κατάξεις ἔθνη. ἀπειλή (*threat*) is substituted for *za'am* (similarly in Prov. xix.12 for *za'ap* also; here it is used for the king's wrath), so that it is no longer the question of an emotional disturbance in God, but of an expression (revelation) of it to the earth. θυμός in the second half of the verse must now be interpreted to correspond. It refers to the will, the intention of God. Hence the meaning given to the sentence by the LXX is like that of Ps. xxxiii.9: *By* (thy mere) *word the earth was made small* (*subject*), *by* (thy mere) *command thou dost overthrow nations*. It is not the God of Sinai, manifesting himself in nature's catastrophes, but the spiritual God who is being praised here. The LXX endeavours to bring out its knowledge of God partly by writing in Deut. xxxii.22 not: *a fire is kindled in my anger* ..., but ἐκ τοῦ θυμοῦ μου, which is probably intended to mean *in consequence of my wrath* or more generally *according to my will*. The LXX has also simply taken over the statements in the Psalms: cf. Ps. ii.12; lxxviii (LXX, lxxvii), 38 (God does not allow his wrath to take full effect); lxxix (LXX, lxxviii), 5; lxxxix (LXX, lxxxviii), 47). Ecclus. xlviii.1 also speaks of God's wrath being mediated. The statement does indeed in the first place refer to Elijah, but from what follows it is clear that it is really God who speaks and acts (verse 3). Thus the passage resembles the prophet's description of the manifestation of God's wrath in Isa. xxx.27; cf. Isa. lxv.5; Jer. iv.4, vii.20, xv.14, xliv [LXX, li], 6. The point of these passages too is the effect brought about by the wrath.[1]

[1] pp. 58 f. are by Bertram.

IV. GOD'S WRATH IN LATE JUDAISM

1. *The Apocrypha and Pseudepigrapha*

THE post-canonical Jewish literature continues on OT lines, in the Diaspora as well as in Palestine.

(*a*) Where the original Hebrew has been preserved (in Ecclus. and in the Zadokite Document [CD]) the words used for wrath (God's) are *'ap* (Ecclus. v.6; CD i.21 [i.17] *et passim*): *ḥēmāh* (Ecclus. xvi.6, 11; xxxvi.6 ; CD ii.5 [ii.4]); *za'am* (Ecclus. v.7, xxxi.23); *rōgez* (Ecclus. v.6). In the Greek texts ὀργή with its derivatives[1] dominates the field as the designation for God's wrath; so too we find θυμός[2] without any material difference of meaning and as the equivalent of the same Hebrew words (obviously preferred in Macc. IV): with θυμόομαι (in the Sibyllines only). The combinations ὀργὴ θυμοῦ (I Macc. ii.49; Gr. Enoch v.9) or θυμὸς καὶ ὀργή (Ecclus. xlv.18) correspond to the duplication *ḥªrōn 'ap* (CD ix.4, 6 [x.2, 4] *et passim*) and are to be considered like similar expressions in Eph. (τὸ κράτος τῆς ἰσχύος in i.19, vi.10, etc.; ἀρχὴ καὶ ἐξουσία in i.21, vi.12, etc.) as a rhetorical piling up of concepts. Other words are rare: ἀγανακτέω in IV Macc. iv.21; παροξύνω Bar. iv.7; Ps. Sol. iv.21; Test. Asher ii.6; χόλος in

---

[1] ὀργίζομαι in Ps. Sol. vii.5; Gr. Enoch xviii.16; Gr. Bar. iv.8, ix.7; Apoc. Mos. viii.16, 18, 21; ἀποργίζομαι in II Macc. v.17; ἐποργίζυμαι in II Macc. vii.23; παροργίζω in Judith viii.14, xi.11; Test. Levi iii.10 *et passim*; παροργισμός Ps. Sol. viii. 9; διοργίζομαι III Macc. iii.1, iv.13.

[2] cf. R. Smend, *Griechisch-syrisch-hebräisches Index zur Weisheit des Jesus Sirach* (1907), s.v. ὀργή and θυμός; cf. p. 74. The range of meaning of θυμός is rather narrower, in so far as it has not shared in the development reaching the meaning of *judgement of wrath* (pp. 63, 87).

Wisdom xviii.22; μηνίω in Prayer of Manasseh 13. The last two with their derivatives are obviously preferred in the epic language of the Sibyllines[1] to ὀργή and θυμός.

(*b*) Wrath in men is considered in a very different light according to whether it is judged from its association with God or whether alien standards are substituted. In the first case it can be considered as a justifiable wrath, if it is kindled by infringement of the law or by blasphemy against God; thus particularly in the Maccabees (I Macc. ii.24, 44; vi.59; II Macc. iv.40; x.35). The wrath of a pagan ruler can also be approved if it is directed against a sinner (cf. II Macc. iv.38; I Macc. ix.69; III Macc. vi.23, cf. p. 75 n. 3); in that case it can even be aroused against God (II Macc. xiii.4; cf. Gr. Bar. xvi.2). The just wrath of a king—as among the Rabbis (cf. p. 68)—serves to illustrate divine anger (Slav. Enoch xlvi.1). According to this view only unrighteous anger is unjustifiable (Ecclus. i.22). But in most cases wrath is condemned as a passion leading to sin and disaster (cf. Wisdom x.2; Ps. Sol. xvi.10; Sib. III.377; CD ix.4, 6 [x.2, 4]); especially in Ecclus. (e.g. x.18, xx.2) and in the XII Testaments (Dan i-vi; Gad v.1; Judah xiv.1; Simeon iv.8; cf. also ii.11; Zebulun iv.11). When frequently disapproval of the fierce rage of the pagan rulers is expressed,[2] this is usually because it is directed against the people of God, but also because it is a sign of the arrogance of man; for in fact wrath befits God alone (Ecclus. x.18). Therefore it is the

---

[1] χόλος in III.51, 556, 561; IV.160, 169; V.130, 373, 456, 508; Fr. 3, 19; χολόομαι in III.766; μηνίω in IV.51; μῆνις IV.135; μήνιμα in III.632, 811; ὀργή in IV.162; V.76; θυμός in III.309; Fr. 3.19; θυμόομαι in V.298, 358.

[2] Tob. i.18; Judith v.2; Ps. Sol. ii.23 f.; xvii.12; Syr. Bar. xlviii.37, lxiii.2; Sib. III.660 f.; and especially also in the books of the Maccabees.

wrath of man which arouses the wrath of God so greatly (Dan. xi.36[1]; Ecclus. v.18 f.; Slav. Enoch xliv.2; Apoc. Abr. xvii (Bonwetsch, p. 28; cf. G. H. Box [1918]), pp. 57 ff.). It is always a sign of God's wrath when he turns away (p. 132); cf. Ecclus. xxviii.3, 5: he who is angry can expect neither ἴασις nor ἐξιλασμός from God; for μῆνις and ὀργή are βδελύγματα in the sight of God (Ecclus. xxvii.30).

When the criteria of reason take precedence over those of religion, wrath is usually condemned (cf. e.g. Ecclus. xxx.24); according to Gr. Enoch (text of Syncellus), viii.3 Semjaza, a leader of the fallen angels, taught men 'to be angry contrary to reason'. Wisdom (x.1 ff.) especially places ὀργή in complete opposition to σοφία. On the other hand in IV Macc. it is significant that θυμός is subordinated to λογισμός (ii.15 ff.) which can cure the former (βοηθῆσαι iii.3). IV Macc. shares with Greek philosophy the problem of mastering wrath (cf. Sen. De Ira II 2, 1 ff.); so does the Letter of Aristeas in the only passage in which it speaks of wrath (253 f.). In addition to the critical and favourable verdicts passed on wrath, the literature contains also many neutral statements about the wrath of man.[2]

(c) In view of the prevailing depreciation of wrath in man, it is striking that almost the whole apocryphal and pseudepigraphical literature speaks without any embarrassment of God's wrath (but cf. p. 65). The only exception, due to its principles, is made by the Letter of Aristeas written under Stoic influence: God rules the

---

[1] The play upon words which is more than that: παροργισθήσεται (i.e. Antiochus IV) . . . ἕως ἂν συντελεσθῇ ἡ ὀργή (i.e. of God) dates only from the Greek translator. Here too postcanonical apocalyptic is merely continuing the line of the canonical apocalypses.

[2] e.g. Tob. v.14; Ecclus. xxv.15; II Esdras x.5, and especially in Jub. (xxvi.8, xxvii. 3, 6, xxviii.4 et passim).

world without wrath of any kind (254).[1] It appears to
be due to chance that Tobit and III Macc. are excep-
tional in making no mention of God's wrath. It is
especially noticeable that a writing so definitely tinged
with Hellenism as IV Macc. reckons quite uncon-
cernedly with the just wrath of God (iv.21, ix.32; p.
65), and that the most passionate delineation of divine
wrath to be found in this literature happens to occur in
the Sibyllines (IV. 59: χόλῳ βρυχῶν).

ὀργή, like θυμός, μῆνις and χόλος with the verbs derived from them, means in the first place the passionate
emotion itself, when for instance the kindling (e.g.
Ecclus. xvi.6) or calming (Ecclus. xlviii.10) of wrath is
mentioned, or when it is said (Eth. Enoch xcix.16): the
Lord *will arouse the spirit of his indignation* (cf. p. 64).
We may call this an 'anthropopathism', but we must
also take into account the fact that it is expressing here
on the one hand God's personal nature,[2] and on the
other his holy abhorrence of all evil. But in not a few
cases ὀργή describes the outcome of divine wrath in its
verdict on man, that is to say, the judgement of wrath,
when for example the great wrath in the Apoc. Mos. xiv
is interpreted as death which dominates our whole race,
or in Vit. Ad. xlix as the catastrophes of water and fire,
falling upon the descendants of Adam and Eve (p. 111),
or when Jub. xxxvi.10 speaks of a daily renewal of the
judgement in wrath and fury. Particularly when ὀργή
is used in the eschatological sense, it often means the
judgement of wrath, thus in Jub. xxiv.30 and especially

[1] This opinion determines also in the subsequent centuries the
Alexandrian tradition in Philo (p. 71), Clement of Alexandria
(p. 7) and Origen (*Cels.* IV.71 ff.).

[2] We can also gather this from the phrase 'to anger the name of
God' (Palaea on Apoc. Abr. xxix, see N. Bonwetsch, *Die Apk.
Abr.* (1897), pp. 63 f.; cf. also p. 63 (top); G. H. Box, *The Apoc. of
Abr.* (1918), pp. 77 f.).

in Gr. Enoch xiii.8: ἴδον ὁράσεις ὀργῆς,[1] as well as in phrases resembling a hendiadys, such as *wrath and punishment* (Eth. Enoch lv.3; xci.7, 9; Jub. xli.26). Often the two ideas can both be detected, namely the upsurge of divine anger and the punishment which it inflicts, thus e.g. in Judith ix.9; I Macc. iii.8; Ecclus. vii.16, xlvii.20; Ps. Sol. xv.4; Test. Reuben iv.8; Test. Levi vi.11; Sib. V.76.[2] This applies especially to some cases in which God's wrath is personified in various ways, as when wrath is said to send (Eth. Enoch ci.3), to go forth (Ecclus. v.7)[3] and to rest (verse 6). But elsewhere personifications of this kind have the direct effect of detaching the reaction of wrath from God himself, thus in Eth. Enoch xcix.16 (the spirit of his indignation); CD ii.5 (ii.4: ḥēmāh gᵉdōlāh as the angel of destruction, cf. p. 69); similarly in Wisdom xviii.22, 25 (wrath as κολάζων and ὀλεθρεύων which Moses resists and conquers).[4] ὀργή as well as denoting the effect of wrath can also describe the occasion for it, as it does obviously in Ecclus. xxvi.8; cf. xxv.22.

The above exposition enables us to recognise the motives for the theodicy. They are also equally evident in the many other statements about God's ὀργή, as for instance in those about the relationship to the mercy, the forbearance and the justice of God (pp. 47f., 87ff.).

---

[1] cf. also Bar. iv.9, 25; I Macc. i.64; Gr. Enoch x.22; Eth. Enoch cvi.15; Ass. Mos. viii.1. A similar meaning must be given in the Sibyllines to χόλος in III.51; V.130 *et passim*) and to μήνιμα (III.811). Even θυμός in Ecclus. xlviii.10, if it is original here, stands clearly for the eschatological judgement.

[2] The same applies to χόλος in Sib. III.556, 561; and θυμός in Ecclus. xviii.24.

[3] cf. also verse 6c, if we should really read ἐλεύσεγαι instead of ἔλεος καί; cf. V. Ryssel in Kautzsch, *Apokryphen und Pseudepigraphen*, I, p. 253.

[4] cf. also the somewhat enigmatic passage in Apoc. Abr. xxv in which God says: *the statue which you saw is my wrath which is aroused in me by the people issuing from you* (i.e. Abraham).

Ecclus. v.6¹ xvi.11 places wrath and mercy side by side as a single quality of God with many tensions: ἔλεος καὶ ὀργὴ παρ' αὐτῷ. It appears similarly in the Prayer of Manasseh 5 f. Particularly with regard to Israel, God's wrath can be seen as the effect of his chastening mercy and love.² This is the way to look at things according to II Macc. v.17, 20, vii.33 and Wisdom xi.9, xvi.5, xviii.20-25 (cf. Ps. Sol. vii.5). On the other hand God's forbearance is shown when he withholds his wrath³ (Syr. Bar. lix.6; cf. Rom. ix.22; pp. 88 f.). God's wrath can be seen too to be in full agreement with the justice when it is kindled by the transgressions of sinners,⁴ indeed it may then be directly called a function of divine justice. This is specially clear in IV Macc. iv.21; cf. ix.32.

Only a few apocalyptists consider that God's justice and mercy exclude the effects of his wrath. II Esdras for instance, in which the image of God is defined on the one hand by passionless justice, on the other by boundless mercy, offers several motives for the restraint of wrath; the small number of the righteous (viii. 30), the ignorance of the masses which resemble the cattle, and the general sinfulness which makes it seem unreasonable and unjust to be angry (viii.34; cf. verse 35).⁵ The

¹ But cf. p. 64, n. 3.
² With regard to the pagans on the other hand an ἀνελεήμων θυμός (Wisdom xix.1) holds sway.
³ cf. by contrast Ecclus. vii.16.
⁴ cf. Sjöberg, pp. 197 f., 224-227.
⁵ II Esdras iv.29 does not belong here, irrespective of a preference for the reading *comminatio* or *indignatio*, because here God's powerful action in cosmic catastrophes is meant (the idea that these are a form of God's judgement of wrath is beside the mark here); Syr. Bar. xxi.6, xlviii.8 is similar (here 'to be angry' appears as the original reading instead of 'to threaten'; Ryssel in *op. cit.* (p. 64, n. 3), II, p. 428 has based his translation on a conjecture of Charles, without indicating this fact). (*Apocrypha and Pseudepigrapha* II (1913), p. 493.)

ideas in Syr. Bar. (xlviii.14, 17) are analogous: the complete frailty and insignificance of man inhibits wrath, although it is uncertain whether this is due to God's justice or to his mercy. In the background of the Apoc. Abr. too there stands the problem of God's justice: why is God angry about the evil which he has himself made subject to his decree? (p. 90).

The wrath of God is discharged in two phases: in the historical and in the eschatological sphere (p. 97).[1] Ecclus. (cf. xviii.24)[2] and the Zadokite Document mention only historical wrath. It falls on all mankind (cf. Eth. Enoch lxxxiv.4; CD ii.21 [iii.7]: on individuals: thus on Cain as the first υἱὸς ὀργῆς[3] (Apoc. Mos. iii),[4] and on Adam and Eve especially (Apoc. Mos. viii f.; Vit. Ad. iii, xxxiv); on individual groups and nations: thus the Egyptians (Wisdom xix.1) or 'the scornful man', 'the man of derision' with his company in the Zadokite Document (i.21 f. [i.17]; v.16 [vii.17], viii.13 [ix.22= Text B, xix.26], viii.18 ix.26]=Text B, xix.31]; on Israel whose chief sin provoking wrath is idolatry (Apoc. Abr. passim; Eth. Enoch lxxxix.33). But whilst God remains angry with others until the end (cf. Wisdom xix.1) in the case of Israel he limits his wrath (cf. xvi.5, xviii.20) and does not destroy utterly (cf. Gr. Enoch v.9: οἱ ἐκλεκτοὶ . . . οὐ μὴ ἀποθάνωσιν ἐν ὀργῇ θυμοῦ); yet cf. Syr. Bar. lxiv.4 and especially Jub. xv.34, where an everlasting wrath even against Israel is mentioned (cf. xxxvi.10). In addition other created things are the objects of his wrath, thus the vine (Gr.

---

[1] Both are denoted side by side by ὀργή and θυμός at random rather than on principle in Ecclus. xlviii.10; but cf. p. 80.

[2] cf. V. Ryssel (p. 64, n. 3) ad loc.

[3] cf. Sib. III.309; Eph. ii.3.

[4] If it is not Cain's wrath against Abel which is meant (the name qain being thought to derive from qānē'); cf. the textual variations in C. Tischendorf, Apocalypses apocryphae (1866), p. 2.

Bar. iv.9) because of its seductive effect,[1] the moon (Gr. Bar. ix.7)[2] and the stars (Gr. Enoch xviii.16); beings hostile to God: the devil (Vit. Ad. xv f.; Jub. iii.23); the hosts of Azazel (Eth. Enoch lv.3), the fallen angels (Gr. Bar. iv. 8; Eth. Enoch lxviii.4: . . . *because they act as if they were the Lord*; Jub. v.6); perhaps the disobedient sons of God of Gen. vi (Gr. Enoch xvi.4, text of Syncellus; xxi.6).[3]

All the operations of wrath within history point forward to the eschatological operation. All the historical periods of wrath (Ecclus. xliv.17; CD i.5 are preludes to *the* day of wrath (e.g. Jub. xxiv.28, 30, xxxvi.10; cf. p. 98), to the ὀργὴ πυρός (Ecclus. xxxvi.8) in the καιρὸς συντελείας (xxxix.28). The eschatological wrath strikes two groups, according to whether the national or the individual aspect predominates. It is directed against the pagans (Ecclus. xxxvi.6; Ass. Mos. x.3; Apoc. Abr. xxiv; probably also Eth. Enoch xc.15, 18; and especially Jub. xxiv.28; here the Philistines are the object of the historical as well as of the eschatological wrath[4]), and against the sinners who do not repent, whether pagans or Israelites, the mighty ones of the earth, on whom the wrath of the Lord of the spirits rests (Eth. Enoch lxii.12), the oppressors of the orphans, widows and strangers (Slav. Enoch l.5 [Text A], etc.; cf. Wisdom v.17–23; Ps. Sol. xv.5; Jub. xxxvi.10, etc.). The very things which appear as the objects of the

---

[1] Another conception, containing an allusion to the Holy Communion, cuts across this one and is probably the result of a Christian interpolation.

[2] According to the Greek text, because the moon shone through the serpent, when Adam was tempted; according to the Slavonic text because the moon laughed when the serpent seduced Adam and Eve and made them conscious of their nakedness.

[3] cf. Stauffer, *Theologie*, p. 199, ET *NT Theology* (1955), pp. 220.

[4] In this 'divine wrath' the Jews give vent to their all too human national wrath.

divine wrath in action in history can also be his tools: men, especially the pagan oppressors and persecutors (IV Macc. iv.21; Ass. Mos. viii.1), various creatures (Wisdom v.22,[1] xvi.5; cf. xi.18), and angels employed against the fallen angels (Jub. v.6).

Judaism too was troubled by the question as to how God's wrath could be overcome and averted; it found a variety of answers, but without knowing the only final one (pp. 129ff.). The answers given are: by prayer (Apoc. Abr. xx [p. 31 Bonwetsch; cf. p. 62; cf. Box, pp. 65 f.]), through services of worship (Slav. Enoch xviii.8 [Text A]; cf. Wisdom xviii.20 ff.), through righteousness (Ecclus. xliv.17), through the vicarious intercession of Moses and Elijah (Wisdom xviii.21; Ecclus. xlviii.10); through vicarious suffering (II Macc. vii.38), through the wrath of the elements, working as an antitoxin (Ecclus. xxxix.28), through God's own saving action (Wisdom xvi.5; Num. xxi). In this last instance Judaism came nearest to the NT; yet it is just here that the veil covering it is clearly seen.

2. *Rabbinic thought*

In the Rabbinic literature too the thought of God's wrath is quite familiar. No trace of any aversion to it can be detected. On the contrary it belongs to those theological matters which are taken for granted. Passages from the OT dealing with God's wrath are quoted without any attempt to re-interpret them. It is often said that God is angry, that he is provoked to wrath, etc. Comparisons are used in which divine wrath is portrayed exactly like that of men; it is described as though a father were angry with his son, a king with his subjects, a husband with his wife.[2] There is no hesitation

[1] Here is a remarkable description of the wrathful God putting on his armour.

[2] cf. e.g. J. Taan. II 65 b 43 (Str.-B. III, p. 30); M. Exod. xiv (Horovitz p. 98); S. Lev. ix.4 f. (Weiss, p. 43a); cf. Sjöberg, p. 63.

here in including in the representations of divine
wrath the irrational quality of chance which charac-
terises human wrath; like the latter, it bursts out perhaps very violently and then after a time it dies down
again;[1] sometimes God is more angry, sometimes less só.[2]
Admittedly these descriptions are tied down to interpretations of biblical passages, but it is worth remarking
that those which might well be omitted are given quite
naturally. All this is the more striking since Rabbinism too
condemns wrath against one's neighbour[3] (although it
recognises that wrath against a sinner is justifiable).[4]

If in some, rather late, passages wrath in various
forms is hypostasised into angels,[5] the reason for it is
definitely, judging by what has been said, not the wish
to avoid anthropopathisms. On the contrary it is due
on the one hand to the preference for a concrete and
vivid method of presentation, peculiar to Rabbinism,
and on the other to the growth of speculations about
angelology in general.

In spite of the freedom with which divine wrath has
been depicted on the pattern of human wrath, Rabbinism asserts firmly on principle that it does not abolish
justice. It is essential to Rabbinism, as to the rest of
Judaism (p. 90) that God never acts contrary to
justice. Thus we read for example on Deut. xxxii.41:
*When I whet my glittering sword, this means, when I deliver the
judgement, it is swift as lightning, but nevertheless* (it is
written) *my hand maintains what is right.*[6]

---

[1] cf. in addition to the passages in the previous note Str.-B. III,
pp. 409, 685, 687.

[2] M. Exod. xvii.4 (Horovitz 174); S. Num. 90 on xi.10. See
also S. Deut. 305 on xxxi.14; R. Nathan: on account of his love
for Israel God will not be angry with their actions.

[3] Str.-B. I, pp. 276 ff.

[4] Str.-B. III, pp. 602 f.; cf. also Str.-B. I, pp. 365 f. (*b* and *c*).

[5] Str.-B. III, pp. 30 f.

[6] S. Deut. 331 on xxxii.41. Cf. Sjöberg, p. 4.

6

In other ways too the wrath of God is distinguished from that of men. An angry man may perhaps strike out in fury having lost control of himself; but God does not forget to care for the world in kindness and mercy even in the hour of his wrath.[1] If sin is in the world, divine wrath is there too[2]; but it is not there alone. Divine mercy is in action also. This means that God does not forget to be kind to the righteous because he is punishing those who provoke his anger. But his mercy is at work for sinners too. It reveals itself especially in forbearance and in good gifts which he bestows on them in spite of their sin, so that there is often occasion to cry: *If God acts thus towards those who provoke him to wrath, how much more will he give to those who do his will?*[3] If he is like this in the hour of wrath, how much more gracious will he be in the hour of good-will.[4]

But the idea that wrath is linked with mercy is by no means always present. Sometimes it is simply said that sin provokes God's wrath and leads to punishment. Occasionally this thought can be carried so far as to say that *sin makes the merciful one* (=God) *cruel.*[5] It holds good particularly at the last judgement, after death or on doomsday, that the sinner will be struck by God's wrath alone without finding mercy.[6] The judgement of

[1] M. Exod. xv.3 (Horovitz, p. 130).

[2] Midr. Tannaim on Deut. xiii.18 (Hoffmann, p. 69); S. Deut. 96 on xiii.18.

[3] See, e.g. M.Exod. xv.1 (Horovitz, pp. 122 f.); xvi.13 (Horovitz, p. 165); S. Deut. 43 on xi.16, 320 on xxxii.19. cf. Sjöberg, pp. 62-71, 86-94, 110-117.

[4] S. Num. 105 on xii.10, 137 on xxvii.14. Here it is speaking of those who are righteous in other respects, but on account of some sin have provoked the wrath of God.

[5] M. Exod. xv.6 (Horovitz, p. 134); S.Num. 175 on xxxi.16.

[6] Mek. R. Sim. on Exod. xx.5 (Hoffmann, p. 105): *A jealous God: This teaches that they saw the figure which in the future will demand requital from the sinners; a jealous God: a God who judges, a hard God, a cruel God.*

Gehenna is a judgement of wrath,[1] and the day of judgement is a day of wrath—although this particular phrase hardly ever occurs.[2] Yet the idea that the judgement is just occupies a much more prominent place than the one that it is executed in wrath.

3. *Philo*

Philo's position between the OT and Stoicism, or rather his attempt to live and to think in both, is reflected also in his statements about wrath. But here too Stoic and Alexandrian ways of thought are in complete control. He admits with biblical and non-biblical antiquity that human wrath against evil and the wrongdoer is justified[3]; but fundamentally he (like the Letter of Aristeas) considers with the Stoics that wrath is an emotion which must be suppressed and controlled by reason.

This makes it intelligible that a certain contradiction appears too in his statements about divine anger: when Philo speaks of ἄξια ὀργῆς he may be thinking of divine as much as of human wrath (*Somn.* II, 179). In such matters it is 'permissible' to speak of God becoming angry[4] and Philo is aware of the real effects of God's wrath on affairs of this earth[5] as well as on the fate of man.[6] Yet on the other hand—and this is the prevailing line in Philo—God's outbursts of wrath are not real—in so far as pagan statements are concerned—but poetical additions,[7] like everything ἀνθρωποπαθές which the pagans attribute to the 'divine' in their poetry (*Sacr. A.C.* 95); for in the case of God there is no real

---

[1] S. Deut. 320 on xxxii.22; see also Str.-B. I, pp. 115 f.

[2] No Rabbinic passage is quoted by Str.-B. III, p. 804 on Rom. ii.5 nor on Rev. vi.17; but cf. p. 98.

[3] cf. Leisegang II, pp. 591 f.

[4] *Somn.* II, 177; cf. also *Spec. Leg.* I, 265.

[5] *Vit. Mos.* I, 6 (of harvest failure in Egypt), cf. also *Vit. Mos.* I, 119.   [6] *Somn.* II, 179.   [7] *Sacr. A.C.* 96.

πάθος.[1] Indeed such features are therefore mere *mythical fictions* (*Deus Imm.* 59). But this interpretation does not hold good in those cases where Moses himself *describes . . . his jealousy, his wrath, his moods of anger, and the other emotions similar to them . . . in terms of human nature* (*Deus Imm.* 60), i.e. with regard to the OT as a whole. The numerous passages in which such things are mentioned in the OT present to Philo a cause of offence and a theological problem. He finally interprets them as an accommodation of the divine word to the receptive capacity of the foolish who are incapable of true knowledge of God; this is a means of helping them to have right ideas[2]; accordingly there is no reality corresponding to such statements, yet they are of value to the learner.[3]

4. *Josephus*

Josephus differs from Philo in that he stands under the influence of the OT and the Rabbinate of his time.[4] Like the LXX he knows ὀργή as both divine and human wrath. In addition he mentions χόλος (e.g. *Bell.* 7, 34, 332), μήνιμα and μῆνις (*Ant.* 15, 243; cf. 15,299), which are found in the LXX almost only in Ecclus. and reveal the influence of Greek thought. On the other hand he never uses θυμός and θυμόομαι,[5] perhaps because θυμός

---

[1] *Abr.* 202: Similarly too Clement of Alexandria, *Strom.* V,11, 68, 3 (cf. the formal identity of expressions with Philo, *Sacr. A.C.* 96; *Somn.* I.285 etc.).

[2] *Deus Imm.* 52. Cf. also Orig. *Cels.* IV.71 f.: to speak of the anger of God is only the Bible's way of speaking for the sake of the uneducated; since what is forbidden to men cannot be ascribed to God.

[3] *Somn.* I, 235. cf. also *Deus Imm.* 53 f. with its contrasting sentences: *God is not as a man—God is as a man* and the appended remark: the first sentence expresses what is real, the second one on the other hand *is introduced for the instruction of many*.

[4] cf. B. Brüne, *Flavius Josephus* (1913), pp. 151-153.

[5] Schlatter, *Theologie des Judentums*, p. 40.

=ḥēmāh did not seem to him to be worthy of God, unless we are to think as with Philo of the psychological meaning of the Platonic θυμός; but this is less likely. He takes over the ὀργὴ θεοῦ from the OT where it is associated with illegal actions and infringements of the law (*Ant.* 11, 141: *lest God conceive anger at all of them alike and again bring misfortune upon them*; 11, 127: *in order that the deity may not conceive any anger against me . . .*, cf. 3, 321: *fear of the law and of the wrath*). In popular opinion the house of Herod stands subject to the divine wrath (*Ant.* 15, 376: *This cannot escape the notice of God, and at the close of your life his wrath will show that he is mindful of these things*; in 15,334: Herod's sickness *had been brought upon them by God in his anger*). Herod's great misfortune in the thirteenth year of his reign seems to be the result of *God's being angry or because misfortune occurs in cycles* (*Ant.* 15, 299); his illness was *just punishment inflicted by God for his lawless deeds* (*Ant.* 17, 168). It is true that Josephus, no doubt under Greek influence, readily replaces the personal ὀργή of God by the impersonal δίκη which 'like εἱμαρμένη (*destiny*) develops into an independent power'.[1] The division into parties in Jerusalem, *being between criminals, might be called a blessing and the work of justice* (*Bell.* 5, 2). When Simon bar Giora was punished it is the case that *villainy does not escape the wrath of God nor is justice weak* (*Bell.* 7, 34). *Simon, in retribution for his cruelty to his fellow-citizens . . . was delivered by God into the hands of his deadliest enemies* (7, 32). Hyrcanus asked the Pharisees *what punishment they thought this man* (Eleazar) *should have . . . in accordance with what was right* (*Ant.* 13, 294). Everywhere belief in God's wrath supplies the foundation, but its limits are set by δίκη; its instrument in Josephus' day is the Romans, whose world power rests on God's plan.

[1] Schlatter, *op. cit.* pp. 40 f. whence the following examples are taken.

V. THE WRATH OF MAN AND THE WRATH OF GOD IN THE NEW TESTAMENT[1]

1. *The wrath of man*

Apart from the root word ὀργή, all derivations from the root ὀργ- are used the in NT to denote only human wrath.[2] Where ὀργή itself is employed in this way it is generally done interchangeably with θυμός (cf. pp. 1; 51 ff.; 80 ff.). Nevertheless, where the sudden blazing passion of wrath and fury is to be described, θυμός is preferred (Luke iv.28; Acts xix.28), although owing to the derivation of ὀργή, it would seem particularly appropriate for just this purpose (cf. p. 1). Yet this word includes an element of set purpose, even of deliberation, which is missing in θυμός; in James i.19 (βραδὺς εἰς ὀργήν) for instance ὀργή could hardly be replaced by θυμός. Παροργίζω and παροργισμός go further than ὀργή and denote the wrathful indignation which threatens to become a lasting bitterness[3]; cf. Eph. vi.4, iv.26, where the change from ὀργίζομαι to παροργισμός is no doubt quite intentional. But elsewhere παροργίζω can be merely the active mood of

[1] In the following pages passages with the synonyms: θυμός, θυμομαχέω, θυμόομαι, ἀγανακτέω, ἀγακάκτηεις, ἐμβριμάομαι, παροξύνομαι, etc., are also taken into consideration in order to go beyond the partly merely fortuitous usage of the words with the stem ὀργ- and to produce as complete a picture as possible of the NT statements concerning human and divine wrath. For detailed discussion of the above words, cf. TWNT *ad loc.*

[2] In the case of ὀργίζομαι in Matt. xviii.34 and xxii.7 human anger is used as a picture of divine wrath; παροργίζω occurs in the NT only twice (in Rom. x.19; Eph. vi.4); παροργισμός and ὀργίλος only once each (Eph. iv.26; Titus i.7). The same applies to θυμόομαι which in the NT is also used for human wrath alone (Matt. ii.16).   [3] cf. Philo, *Somn.* II, 177.

ὀργίζομαι (as in Rom. x.19), as it usually is in its frequent use in the LXX.

i. *The conditional justification for wrath in man*

In the NT there is no uniform opinion on the question of man's giving way to anger. It differs from Stoicism (cf. pp. 2 f.), because a complete condemnation of human wrath is not possible where the wrath of God receives serious consideration. For if every stirring of wrath is automatically condemned, then statements about God's wrath must be explained away.[1] But if on the contrary these statements are taken seriously, then in the human sphere too at least a certain limited right to wrath must be recognised (yet cf. Rom. xii.19; cf. pp. 78, 104). The NT is acquainted with a holy wrath, hating what God hates, and demonstrates it most of all by Jesus himself (Mark iii.5: μετ' ὀργῆς; cf. John xi.33, 38, both times ἐμβριμᾶσθαι; cf. Paul in Acts xvii.6: παρωξύνετο τὸ πνεῦμα αὐτοῦ ἐν αὐτῷ). When Jesus is angry God's own wrath manifests itself (cf. pp. 92 ff.). Yet whilst this wrath, simply by reason of its close association with derivatives from the root δικ-[2] (Rom. i.18, iii.5, xii.19, xiii.4) appears as a δικαία ὀργή (cf. pp. 2, 90), human wrath is never described in the NT by this word.[3] Wrath is God's right; but it is not right for man (James i.20; cf. p. 77).[4] Whilst God's love

---

[1] As is done in Stoicism (cf. p. 5), Philo (cf. p. 71). Origen (*Cels*. IV, 71 ff.), etc.

[2] *Righteousness* in this series (1951, 1959), esp. pp. 13 ff.

[3] On the other hand instances of just wrath are found amongst the Greeks (cf. p. 2), in the OT (cf. p. 18) and amongst the Jews. In the last case it is found not only towards the ungodly (cf. the passages in Str-B. III, pp. 602 f.), but also—according to the Jewish attitude towards the alien (cf. TWNT V, pp. 11 ff.) —towards non-Jews (cf. S. Lev. xix.18 (352a) in Str-B I, p. 366).

[4] Something similar may be said of ἐπιτιμᾶν (cf. TWNT II, pp. 620 ff.), one of the forms in which ὀργή expresses itself.

includes wrath (cf. pp. 87 f.), in man love and wrath exclude each other (cf. I Cor. xiii.5: ἀγάπη . . . οὐ παροξύνεται). Only in two passages in the NT does human wrath appear as having a definite value. In Rom. x.19: ἐπ' ἔθνει ἀσυνέτῳ παροργιῶ ὑμᾶς. This παροργισμός differs in meaning from its use in the passage quoted there (Deut. xxxii.21)[1] by being a salutary wrath; God himself brings it about in order to move Israel to self-examination. In II Cor. vii.11 ἀγανάκτησις (only here in the NT) stands beside ἐκδίκησις amongst the seven fruits of repentance and clearly denotes the well-founded wrathful indignation over the ἀδικήσας (verse 12) or their own attitude which hitherto has been so mistaken.[2]

ii. The condemnation of human wrath

Everywhere else in the NT the wrath of man is condemned. We can see this already in the gloomy pictures of the angry man (wherever Christ or God himself is not meant, cf. pp. 95 ff.), in the parables, stories and visions of the NT, e.g. in that of the elder brother in Luke xv.28. Here is the antithesis of Jesus, for his anger is merciless as contrasted with holy merciful wrath (Mark iii.5). God's wrath is that of wounded love (cf. pp. 88, 124, 95), man's wrath is that of indignant selfishness (cf. Luke iv.28).

Selfish wrath such as this is necessarily directed against God, as it is in Luke xv.28 (apart from the very transparent imagery here) and in iv.28 (ἐπλήσθησαν πάντες θυμοῦ) and it is especially so in the case of the Gentiles (Rev. xi.18; cf. Acts xix.28: γενόμενοι πλήρεις

[1] cf. also Ezek. xxxii.9 and especially Gr. Bar. xvi, a passage perhaps interpolated from Rom.x.19. But here the helpless anger of the Jews is not shown the prospect given by Paul, that it will be the means of leading them back to God.

[2] cf. H. Windisch, Kommentar z. 2. Korintherbrief (⁹1924) ad loc.

θυμοῦ; Heb. xi.27: [Moses] μὴ φοβηθεὶς τὸν θυμὸν τοῦ βασιλέως). The final concentration of anger against God is that of the devil (Rev. xii.17; cf. verse 12: ἔχων θυμὸν μέγαν); he is full of fury with God's victorious preparations for salvation[1] and at the same time because his own scheme for damnation has been defeated. The historical antitype to the wrathful devil is Herod (Matt. ii.16: ἐθυμώθη λίαν), likewise because his scheme, intended to frustrate God's plan of salvation, proved unsuccessful.[2] These concealed causes of hostility to God constitute a main reason for Jesus' verdict, like that in James i.20: ὀργὴ . . . ἀνδρὸς δικαιοσύνην θεοῦ οὐκ ἐργάζεται i.e. the angry man cannot stand before God. Perhaps we can understand Jesus' saying about being angry in the Sermon on the Mount (Matt. v.22: πᾶς ὁ ὀργιζόμενος τῷ ἀδελφῷ αὐτοῦ ἔνοχος ἔσται τῇ κρίσει in this sense, if verse 22b and c were added only later; in that case ἔνοχος τῇ κρίσει means to *come under the final judgement of God*. But since the tripartite logion must for several reasons be considered genuine, κρίσις must be given the meaning of the *local court of justice*, and the logion itself receives the grotesque quality characteristic of so many sayings in the Sermon on the Mount. For what human judge can indict anger before his court, unless it has incriminated itself by concrete expressions (as some people have indeed conjectured to be Jesus' meaning)? But it is just this grotesque quality which shows—as elsewhere too—the absolute nature of Jesus' demands. Anger which has not yet made itself known even by a word is put on a par with homicide; anger is

[1] The wrath of the devil with the attempts of the first men to recover their salvation is a kind of prototype (*Life of Adam and Eve*, ix).

[2] The NT shows us another furious Herod (Acts xii.20), though without explaining the reason of his θυμομαχεῖν. If we might connect it with the immediately preceding narrative, then here too it would represent wrath at the failure of a godless plan.

the first step in murder.[1] Jesus, even more than OT
(cf. p. 21) attributes to ὀργή the full seriousness of sin.
Paul too and his followers share this view. In Col.
iii.8 and Eph. iv.31 ὀργή is included in the condemnation of the κακία, and in fact here again, as in James
i.19 (beside λαλῆσαι), it is clearly chiefly a sin of the
tongue.[2] Whilst refraining from wrath is called giving
place to God (Rom. xii.19),[3] being angry leads to
giving an opportunity to the devil (Eph. iv.26 f.).
Indeed if it grows into revenge it becomes an usurpa-
tion of God's exercise of his wrath (cf. p. 104) and of his
rights as a judge (Rom. xii.19). The anger of man is
therefore met by the wrath of God (cf. Col. iii.8 with
verse 6 and especially Rev. xi.18; cf. p. 118)[4] in the
time of the judgement.[5] Hence the exhortation not to
be angry oneself (Col. iii.8; Eph. iv.31, cf. p. 2) nor
to provoke others to anger (Eph. vi.4); for that means
leading them into sin (σκανδαλίζειν) and this is just as
bad as ἁμαρτάνειν or even worse (cf. Matt. xviii.6).
Anger is therefore banished particularly from the
proximity of God, thus in I Tim. ii.8: βούλομαι . . .

---

[1] cf. amongst others H. Huber, *Die Bergpredigt* (1932), pp. 76-
85.

[2] Similarly θυμοί in Gal. v.20 belong to the ἔργα τῆς σαρκός
and in II Cor. xii.20 to the catalogue of vices, for the most part
sins of the tongue. These statements differ in this respect from
Matt. v.22 where ὀργή and sins of the tongue are clearly distinguished.

[3] Rom. xii.19 is completed by I Peter ii.23 which uses Jesus as
an example in accordance with his own words in Matt. v.38 ff., 44.

[4] A good parallel is found in Livy 8, 6, 2 f.: Annius is angry
with Jupiter and in consequence he is himself slain by the wrath
of the gods.

[5] The same thought occurs in B. Ned. 22a (in Str.-B. I, p. 277):
He who is angry is subject to all the punishments of Gehenna; for
Gehenna is the place of the judgement of wrath. Conversely
according to Gr. Bar. xvi when God becomes angry man replies by
getting angry too.

προσεύχεσθαι τοὺς ἄνδρας ... χωρὶς ὀργῆς καὶ διαλογισμοῦ[1];
Titus i.7: δεῖ ... τὸν ἐπίσκοπον ἀνέγκλητον εἶναι ... μὴ
αὐθάδη, μὴ ὀργίλον. If a man is θεοῦ οἰκονόμος (of the
household of God), wrath is not compatible with the service in the sanctuary,[2] for where wrath is found God
does not wish to dwell (Ign. Phld. viii.1).

This almost general condemnation of wrath in man
explains the greater reserve adopted by the NT than by
its environment towards concessions which can be
found at most in Eph. iv.26 and James i.19. In Eph.
iv.26 (ὀργίζεσθε καὶ μὴ ἁμαρτάνετε) ὀργίζεσθε does not
have the full emphasis of the imperative, not merely
because it is a quotation (Ps. iv.5) but because it is
given in the rendering of the LXX;[3] i.e. instead of be
angry so far as I am concerned, but do not sin, it would be
better to render it if you must be angry, beware lest you sin.
Anger is not actually called sin, but the thought is
suggested; when a man is angry, sin lies in wait at the
door.[4] So it goes on to say: ὁ ἥλιος μὴ ἐπιδυέτω ἐπὶ
παροργισμῷ ὑμῶν. This quotation must also be read in
the light of the saying which follows 5 verses later (verse

---

[1] In the case of ὀργή, as well as in that of διαλογισμός, it is
open to question whether it is directed against God (cf. Plut.
De Ira Cohibenda 5 (II, 455d; cf. p. 2): we are angry even with the
gods) or against men. In the latter case it would be parallel to
Mark xi.25 (cf. Matt. v.23 f.). The rabbinic parallels (in Str.-B.
III, p. 643) make the latter more probable at any rate in the case
of ὀργή (thus also G. Wohlenberg, Kommentar z. d. Pastoralbriefen
(1906), p. 112.

[2] In substance Ign. Phld. i.2 says the same thing: his incapacity
for anger (i.e. of the bishop). But the word is in the neuter and the
related expressions (steadfastness, virtuous, reasonableness: τὸ
ἀνίκητον, ἐνάρετος, ἐπιείκεια) suggest the influence of Stoicism
on the ideas; cf. W. Bauer in Handbuch z. NT, Die Apostolischen
Väter (1923) ad loc.

[3] For other renderings see Str.-B. III, p. 602.

[4] The thought in B. Ber. 29b is similar; Do not flare up, lest you
sin, etc.

31), in which πᾶσα ὀργή is rejected. The continuation
quoted above (Eph. iv.26b) forms a counterpart to
James i.19: ἔστω δὲ πᾶς ἄνθρωπος . . . βραδὺς εἰς ὀργήν
(cf. verse 20), inasmuch as here too wrath is not rejected absolutely to start with and the thoughts in the
two passages complete each other: first, take a long
time before you allow yourself to be angry (James), and
then, do not take long in suppressing your anger (Eph.)[1]
The phrase βραδὺς εἰς ὀργήν might be considered as the
parallel and equivalent of *longsuffering* ('*erek* '*appaim*)
beside μακρόθυμος (cf. pp. 22, 103). In that case this
would be a recommendation for the imitation of God
and his longsuffering, and since this is very similar to
his grace (cf. pp. 88 f.) this exhortation would approximate to the demand to forgive instead of being angry.
Here too, as in Eph. iv, the apparent concession is
followed by the sentence in verse 20 already quoted
above: *for the anger of man does not work the righteousness of
God.*[2]

2. The wrath of God

i. Differences from contemporary usage

(a) Linguistic differences. Unlike Josephus,[3] but
certainly following the lead of the LXX,[4] the NT never

[1] This behaviour is practised in both senses by those who *hold
righteous indignation in reserve*, the phrase used in praise of the Essenes
by Josephus in *Bell*. 2, 135.

[2] For the meaning of δικαιοσύνη θεοῦ in this passage, cf. Pirke
Abot v.11: (*He who is*) *hard to provoke and easy to pacify, he is pious.*
When considering expressions like this, one should picture to
oneself how different were the conditions in vogue at that time
outside the world of those thinking in biblical categories (cf.
Athenag. Suppl. 21). On the one hand concern for culture, on
the other for righteousness and piety; on the one hand concern
for men, on the other for God.

[3] cf. A. Schlatter, *Wie sprach Josephus von Gott?* (1910), p. 59.

[4] cf. Wetter, p. 16.

employs μῆνις[1] and χόγος,[2] terms used in Greek poetry for the inexorable wrath of the gods (cf. pp. 2 f., but it denotes God's anger only by ὀργή and θυμός,[3] θυμός appearing only in Rom. ii.8 and in Revelation (xiv.10, 19; xv.1, 7; xvi. 1, 19; xix.15).[4]

It cannot be decided confidently whether a feeling for the difference in quality between θυμός and ὀργή influenced the apostle Paul or the seer John in their choice of words.[5] The piling up of concepts in several of these passages (Rom. ii.8 f.: ὀργή καὶ θυμὸς,[6] θλῖψις καὶ στενοχωρία; Rev. xvi.19: τὸ ποτήριον τοῦ οἴνου τοῦ θυμοῦ τῆς ὀργῆς; similarly xix.15; xiv.10), serving to increase the shattering impression of the tremendous reality of divine wrath (cf. pp. 23, 60), does not permit a more precise differentiation in the meaning between θυμός and ὀργή. But it might perhaps be said that θυμός, to which clings the concept of passion breaking out, is well suited to represent the vision of the seer, but not to denote the Pauline conception of God's wrath.

[1] But the LXX does used the verb μηνίζω (μηνίω) for God as well, e.g. Ps. ciii.9 [LXX, cii.9].

[2] But significantly in Sib. VIII.93 *(inexorable)*.

[3] cf. von Jüchen, pp. 49 f. The reason for this may be purely linguistic, namely, that already at that time the other terms were felt to be predominantly poetic and strange in prose. On the other hand it may be due not so much to the fact that these words have lost their forcefulness (cf. Wetter, p. 16) as because the conception and the understanding of the difference between the wrath of the gods and that of God had become clarified.

[4] cf. TWNT III, pp. 168, 7 ff. For the use of derivatives, cf. p. 74 and n. 2; also pp. 54 f.

[5] cf. pp. 1 f. and on this especially also Philodemus, *De Ira*, 32 ff. (Wilke, p. 90), as well as the passages quoted in the apparatus there about the meaning of ὀργή and the difference between ὀργή and θυμός. Cf. also Trench, pp. 123 ff.

[6] So also Aelianus, *Var. Hist.* 13, 2 (in A. Fridrichsen, 'Observationen zum NT aus Ael. *Var. Hist.*': Symbolae Osloenses 5 (1927), p. 63); Isoc. 12, 81, etc.

The meaning of ὀργή can be defined more exactly by observing the terms with which it is used together or in contrast in the NT (cf. p. 98). The fact that it stands beside ἐκδίκησις (Luke xxi.22; Rom. ii.5; cf. TWNT II, pp. 442 ff.) and δικαιοκρισία (Rom. ii.5) (cf. p. 75; cf. TWNT II, p. 229; *Righteousness* in this series [1951], p. 73) excludes the idea of unbridled and therefore unjust vengeance when it is applied to God. That it has as parallels θλῖψις (Mark xiii.19 and par.; Rom. ii.8 f.), στενοχωρία (Rom. ii.8 f.) and ἀνάγκη (Luke xxi.23) shows that in the majority of the NT passages the effect of the wrath rather than the emotion itself predominates in the meaning of the word (p. 87; cf. pp. 26 f.).

(b) Differences in meaning

Jesus and the Baptist (Luke iii.18) bring a gospel which includes the announcement of the ὀργὴ θεοῦ (cf. Matt. iii.7 and par.; Luke xxi.23), and like them Paul, the Gospel and the Revelation of John testify to a message which proclaims not only the grace and mercy, but also the wrath of God (cf. e.g. Rom. i.18; John iii.36; Rev. xiv.10). The wrath of God is therefore to be regarded by no means as a piece of the OT religion of the law, dragged in as an irrelevance, as though speaking of God's anger belonged by its nature to the OT, whilst speaking of his love similarly belonged exclusively to the NT. For the OT proclaims the love and the mercy of God beside his wrath as impressively as the NT preaches the wrath of God together with his mercy (cf. pp. 87 f.).

Although the world into which the men of the NT were born and that to which they spoke regarded the wrath of God as something to be reckoned with, yet the NT is in this respect characteristically distinguished from the values of the world before their time and of that surrounding them. It is true that a profound cause of divine wrath is the same in both, namely the *hubris* of men which fundamentally despises God and at any rate wants to live its life without him (cf. Rom. ii.4 ff., i.18 ff.; cf. pp. 101, 104). But when in the pagan world everlasting enmity appears in consequence between gods and men,[1] there remains in the NT beside and above the wrath the love of God, and its wounding continually supplies fresh occasions for his wrath (cf. p. 76). It is in accordance with this that nowhere in the NT is God's wrath described with the colouring of psychic or natural passion, which appears so frequently in the OT. The NT does not contain any trace of those enigmatic, irrational outbursts of wrath, and the divine wrath does not burn for ever (cf. pp. 105 ff.). In the NT a theological concept of ὀργή clearly outweighs the psychological one.[2] Closely associated with this is the fact that consideration of the effect plays a larger part in the NT than consideration of the 'psychic reaction' (cf. p. 103).

ii. *The place of wrath in the NT conception of God*

(*a*) In the biblical conception of God, and hence in that of the NT as well, wrath is an essential feature which cannot be omitted. Behind all the passages—and this applies to the whole NT—which are aware that it is a terrible thing to fall into the hands of the living God (Heb. x.31), that he is able to save life and to destroy it (James iv.12), and that he is feared because after he has killed he has authority to cast into hell (Luke

---

[1] cf. von Jüchen, pp. 33, 47 f.

[2] This is shown in phrases such as ἐπιφέρω ὀργήν (Rom. iii.5), ὀργὴ ἔρχεται (Rev. xi.18) or φθάνει (I Thess. ii.16), θησαυρίζω ὀργήν (Rom. ii.5), etc.; cf. Pohlenz, p. 14.

xii.5; Matt. x.28),[1] there lies the awareness of God's wrath.[2]

(b) At times in the NT also wrath does seem (pp. 24, 69) to be, as it were, detached from God, like an independent active power, indeed almost personified as a terrible demon. It is undoubtedly striking that Paul in 15 out of 18 passages speaks of ὀργή without the qualification (τοῦ) θεοῦ.[3] A theory based on this and some other observations[4] has been propounded that Paul, like Judaism, considers ὀργή to be an independent being standing beside God.

Traces of such an 'absolute' usage of ὀργή occur already in the OT (cf. Ezra vii.23; Dan. viii.19). The personification of ὀργή was also prepared for in the OT by the simile of the *weapons of wrath* (Isa. xiii.5; Jer. l.25; cf. p. 32),[5] as well as by all kinds of figurative

---

[1] It seems to me that there can be no doubt that in this logion Jesus is thinking not of the devils but of God; cf. the commentaries *ad. loc.*

[2] In some passages this wrath seems to have 'numinous' features (e.g. Mark xi.14; Heb. xii. 29). Thus Otto, pp. 99 ff. (ET, pp. 88 ff.) attempts to fit a series of NT passages and narratives, particularly that of Gethsemane (cf. p. 131 and p. 114 n. 2), into the picture sketched by him of the phenomenon of numinous wrath. But there is no room either in the portrayal of Jesus or of God in the NT for divine wrath as an irrational, *mysterium tremendum*. Besides, in all passages of this kind the real subject under consideration is the holy wrath of Jesus Christ and of his father (cf. P. Althaus, *Die christliche Wahrheit* II (1948), p. 163.

[3] Some textual witnesses supply the θεοῦ which they find missing in several passages: Western evidence in I Thess. ii.16, Chrysostom on Rom. xii.19. By contrast, Marcion suppresses the genitive in Rom. i.18, because it does not fit into his image of God.

[4] cf. Wetter, pp. 16-55; the same is hinted at also in Pohlenz, p. 15. Böhmer, pp. 320-322 discusses the same observations and similar conclusions with regard to the OT.

[5] Hebrew: *keˡlē zaʿam*, LXX Jer. xxvii.25 (= l.25 in the Masoretic text): σκεύη ὀργῆς, clearly weapons which God takes out of his armoury (θησαυρός); cf. also Isa. x.5: ῥάβδος τοῦ θυμοῦ μου

phrases, as for example, the sending, coming, passing over of wrath (e.g. Isa. x.6, xxvi.20; cf. p. 64), or when God says in Isa. lxiii.5: *my wrath upheld me*. But Judaism goes appreciably further on this road, as already in numerous passages in the Apocrypha and Pseudepigrapha (cf. Wisdom xviii.21: [Moses] ἀντέστη τῷ θωμῷ). Apoc. Abr. xxv speaks in a rather enigmatic manner of a statue of God's wrath[1] *with which the people issuing from thee* (i.e. Abraham) *and coming to me provoke me*. For Rabbinic Judaism 'the wrath' is one of the two fundamental forces (*Middoth*) associated with God.[2] On the other hand *'ap* and *ḥēmāh* or the angel of wrath (*mal'ak za'ap*)[3] appear as independent angels of destruction (cf. p. 103 n. 2; p. 64). On the one hand it is thought that the 'absolute' construction of ὀργή in the NT may be recognised as a continuation along this line; on the other hand it is seen as a form of the fatalism of antiquity, a counterpart to the εἰμαρμένη (*destiny*) of the Greeks and the *Fatum* of the Romans, although it is

καὶ ὀργῆς. But in Isa. xiii.5 the LXX renders *kᵉlē za'am* which figure in God's battle-array at the judgement of the world by ὁπλομάχοι. For the whole question, cf. Böhmer, pp. 320 ff.

[1] Obviously the 'statue' stands till the end as a memorial of the judge, for the human sacrifices to idols are called a *witness to the last judgement*.

[2] cf. Bousset-Gressmann, pp. 350 f. 'Wrath' corresponds to *quality of justice (middat haddīn)*. According to S.Num. 71a; Targum Ps. lvi.11 and other passages, the name Elohim belongs to this, whilst the name Yahweh belongs to *quality of mercy (middat hāraḥᵃmīm)*; cf. also Weber, pp. 145, 259. In the light of this conception, it is not only possible, but significant that the Midrash reads Ps. vii.6 [Heb. 7] in the form: *Arise, Yahweh, against thy wrath*, (instead of *in thy wrath*) and that in B. Ber. 7a God is said 'to pray': *May it be my will that my mercy may restrain my wrath*.

[3] cf. B. Shab. 55a; Deut. R. 3 (200c). J. Taan. 2, 65b 43 (cf. p. 103) in Str.-B. III, pp. 30 f.; cf. Bousset-Gressmann, pp. 350 f.; Weber, pp. 154, 172; Böhmer, p. 321.—Tanch. 155b (in Str.-B. III, p. 30).

7

admitted that the ὀργή of the NT differs from these deities of fate by the fact that it is always subject to God and guided by him.[1]

It must be stated in contradistinction to these alleged prototypes and counterparts of the NT ὀργή that (1) the conception of transcendent personifications of wrath (such as the prophets' *weapons of wrath* (cf. pp. 32, 108 f.) or the angels of wrath) is unknown to the NT; for the angels in the book of Revelation who pour out the bowls of wrath, etc., are merely messengers and those who carry out God's will in accordance with the nature of all the angels in the NT. (2) Although the coming of the wrath (yet never its sending, etc.) is mentioned several times in the NT, yet the *coming* in this context is merely a technical term for the coming of that which is to come, i.e. the last things.[2] (3) The NT has nothing to do with two basic motifs of the religiosity of that period, namely fatalism and dualism. It can easily be demonstrated that in none of the NT passages is ὀργή a rigid principle acting independently of God, but that it stands everywhere in the closest connection with him and in fact with the God whose personal reaction it is.[3] It must not be concluded from the fact that θεοῦ is frequently lacking that ὀργή is felt even by Paul to be an independent hypostasis. On the contrary this usage enables the power to be recognised which makes all men conscious of God.[4] The independent use of ὀργή is altogether in line with that of χάρις in Paul and his successors[5] who likewise take for granted its meaning of God's grace.

[1] Wetter, pp. 46-55.

[2] cf. Cr. Kö. pp. 445 f. *sv*; TWNT II, pp. 666 ff.

[3] cf. Braun, p. 42.

[4] Thus A. Schlatter, *Kommentar 2. Matthäusev.* (1929), p. 71.

[5] cf. especially Rom. v.20 f., vi.14 f.; Phil. i.7; Heb. iv.16; also, e.g. in the (introductions and) endings of the letters; thus in I Peter i.2; Col. iv.18; I Tim. vi.21; II Tim.iv.22; Heb. xiii.25.

(c) But in spite of the fact that the NT ὀργή cannot be detached from God, we must not dismiss the question: does this idea really imply the idea of an emotional disturbance in God (cf. p. 26)? Is it not rather the act of punishment inflicted by God in his wrath?[1] (cf. pp. 2, 63, 82). Now Origen (*Cels.* IV, 72) is undoubtedly right: a passion cannot be 'stored up' (Rom. ii.5 f.). In most of the NT passages ὀργή is in fact the working out of God's wrath, its infliction and its judgement (thus in Matt. iii.7 and par.; Rom. ii.5, xii.19, etc.). But it cannot be denied that some NT passages using ὀργή imply the conception of an actual divine behaviour, just as it is possible that they do in the case of ἀγάπη[2] and ἔλεος;[3] so in Rom. i.18, ix.22; Rev. vi.16 and most definitely in the quotation from the OT in Heb. iii.11, iv.3. As in the OT (cf. p. 32), so also in the NT ὀργή is both things: God's indignation at evil, his 'passionate' aversion to all wills which are contrary to him,[4] as well as his intervention in judgement on them.

(d) Objections have been raised again and again to the assertion that the ὀργὴ θεοῦ is an integral part of the biblical message. This is based particularly on the belief in God's love. It is said that if God really is love, surely he cannot be angry.[5] But already the period

[1] Thus R. Bultmann, pp. 283 f. (ET pp. 288 f.).

[2] cf. *Love* in this series (1949), esp. pp. 54 ff.

[3] cf. Althaus, *op. cit.* (cf. p. 84 n. 2), II, p. 164.

[4] cf. P. Kalweit, article on 'Zorn Gottes' in RGG [2]V, 2137. In the Enlightenment, such conceptions were called 'crude anthropopathisms of an uneducated age' (quoted by Ruegg in RE[3] 21, p. 719). But they are in no way more anthropopathic than the biblical statements about God's love as a father; they all belong inseparably to the biblical image of a personal God.

[5] This conclusion was drawn, e.g. already by Marcion for his 'good God'; cf. Tertullian, Marc. I. 27: *Deus melior inventus est, qui nec offenditur nec irascitur nec ulciscitur. (He discovered a better god, who is neither offended, nor does he get angry, nor does he take vengeance.)*

before the NT knew that in God wrath and love do not exclude each other, but in fact include each other.[1] In the NT as in the OT, in the case of Jesus as in that of the prophets, in the case of the apostles as in that of the rabbis, the preaching of God's mercy is accompanied by the announcement of God's wrath (cf. p. 82). Only he who knows the greatness of the wrath is overwhelmed by the greatness of the compassion. Again it is equally true that only he who has experienced the greatness of the compassion can realise how great the wrath must be. For God's wrath springs out of his love and his compassion (cf. p. 39): where this compassion encounters man's hostile will instead of faith and gratitude, good will and answering love, then love is turned into wrath (cf. Matt. xviii.34; Mark iii.5; Rom. ii.5). Christ is the touch-stone which divides mankind into those who are exempt from wrath because they have allowed themselves to be rescued by his compassion, and those who remain under wrath because they scorn his compassion. Simeon (Luke ii.34) and John the Baptist (Matt. iii.12) had announced this about Jesus from the outset. This was the effect of his words and actions, as he himself had seen (cf. Luke xx.18; Mark iv.12); and at the last by dying between the two criminals he demonstrated in his own person this divisive power for all to see (Luke xxiii.39 ff.).

(e) How is the ὀργή related to God's forbearance (μακροθυμία, cf. TWNT IV, pp. 378 f.)? This becomes the burning question in the exegesis of Rom. ix.22: εἰ δὲ θέλων ὁ θεὸς ἐνείξασθαι τὴν ὀργὴν κτλ. The

[1] cf. Prayer of Manasseh 5 f. The same is summed up twice over more tersely in Ecclus. v.6 = xvi.11 (in the second passage at least the text must be considered original owing to the parallel in the other half of the verse, cf. pp. 64 f., n. 3). For a more recent discussion, cf. K. Barth, *Kirchliche Dogmatik*, II, 1 ([2]1946), pp. 407, 442-446; ET, *Church Dogmatics*, II, 1 (1957). Althaus, *op. cit.* (p. 84, n. 2), II, pp. 32 f.

forbearance of God appears in a somewhat different light according to whether θέλων is taken here to be causative[1] or concessive.[2] Is it a servant of his wrath or a means of his compassion? Probably it has a double function: it is primarily the outpouring of love (cf. I Cor. xiii.4) and of pity, giving the sinner time for repentance (cf. Rom. ii.4; Rev. ii.21; II Peter iii.9) and consequently an aid to salvation (II Peter iii.15; cf. I Tim. i.16) whereby even the σκεύη ὀργῆς can become σκεύη ἐλέους[3] and thus it is a way to the final manifestation of the glory for the vessels of mercy. But when the patience of God is slighted and misused (cf. I Peter iii.20), it serves merely to increase the divine wrath and to render more certain the perdition to which the σκεύη ὀργῆς are destined (cf. Ign. Eph. xi.1). God's forbearance has the same mysterious twofold effect as all demonstrations of God's grace—e.g. the miracles of healing and Jesus' parables, even Jesus himself (cf. p. 97). They cause some to fall, others to rise again. Thus we may paraphrase Rom. ix.22 as follows: *But if God bore with great forbearance with the vessels of wrath, created for destruction, because he wished to use them for demonstrating his wrath and making known his power (yet he did this) nevertheless also[4] in order that he might make known the riches*

[1] Zahn, Schlatter, Kühl, Lietzmann, Althaus, etc.

[2] Thus B. Weiss, *Römerbrief* ([9]1893), *ad loc.* A. Jülicher in *Schriften des NT*, ed. J. Weiss ([3]1917 *ff.*) *ad loc.* and the translations of Weizsäcker, Menge, the Zürich Bible, etc. Cf. here text and margin of NEB.

[3] The possibility which repentance turns into reality is open to the σκεύη ὀργῆς just as much as for the τέκνα φύσει ὀργῆς. See Eph. ii.3 (cf. pp. 109 f.). The NT knows of no rigid predestination to eternal perdition (cf. p. 109, n. 2). On this particular matter another view is held by T. Zahn, *Römerbrief* (1910), p. 459 (but cf. p. 461), H. Lietzmann, *Römerbrief* ([3]1928) on ix.22, etc. (cf. p. 90, n. 1).

[4] καί is lacking here in B Vulg. etc.; if it is understood as *also* the construction is difficult but not impossible. So too T. Zahn,

of his glory through the vessels of his grace which he had pre-
pared for glory long ago. Here too the idea of Rom. i.17 f.
and iii.23 lies in the background, that the manifestation
of wrath is the indispensable foil for the manifestation of
grace.[1]

(*f*) The tension between wrath and justice, with
which antiquity was acquainted in spite of the fact that
the judge was permitted on principle to display wrath,[2]
reveals its own special set of problems in the theological
thought of the NT. Here God's wrath dominates the
sin of mankind, but it is just the ἀδικία of men which
actually promotes the triumph of his δικαιοσύνη[3] (Rom.
iii.4 f. ὅπως). If there were no sin there could not be the
miracle of the *sola gratia*, on which not only our salvation, but also God's glory depend (verse 7). Hence the
question seems to be justified (Rom. iii.5): μὴ ἄδικος ὁ
θεὸς ὁ ἐπιφέρων τὴν ὀργήν; indeed when the inter-
weaving of causes and of effects in the working of ὀργή
is examined more closely, it becomes necessary to amplify
the question: Is it right for God to be angry with the
chaos of sin into which he himself thrusts God-forgotten
mankind[4] (cf. pp. 120, 126 f., 128 f.). Paul's answer to
these questions is to begin with (Rom. iii.6) an argument

Römerbrief (1910), p. 458, n. 24; P. Althaus, *Römerbrief* (NTD) *ad
loc.*, etc.

[1] A somewhat different interpretation in J. Chr. K. von Hofmann,
Die heilige Schrift NTs III (1868), pp. 401-406 and cf. TWNT
IV, pp. 377 ff. (Horst); especially p. 385; both reject the possi-
bility considered in p. 89, n. 3.

[2] cf. p. 2; Pohlenz, p. 15, n. 3 and Hirzel, p. 417 refer to
Demosth. 24.118 and Aeschines 3.197, where there is a discussion
of the manner in which the offence can be matched with the
judge's wrath.

[3] cf *Righteousness* in this series (1951), esp. pp. 40 ff.

[4] cf. Apoc. Abr. xxvii (Bonwetsch, p. 36) with xxv (p. 35) where
the metaphor of God's wrath with Israel passes over unnoticed
into the idol with which Israel arouses God's wrath; i.e. God's
wrath always produces fresh wrath (cf. pp. 126 f.).

of Jewish theology: God is the judge of the world; thus he cannot be other than just. Today we should modify this argument somewhat as follows: When a man knows himself to be a sinner who deserves to receive from God nothing but wrath, from the final judgement nothing but condemnation, he sees that God's judgement is raised high above all questionings; for he recognises that God's wrath, being his repugnance against unrighteousness is simply an expression of his righteousness.[1]

This idea is already the basis of Paul's exposition in Rom. i.18 ff. But the introductory parallelism of verses 17 and 18 contains a quite different answer to this question, expressing an astonishing agreement between God's wrath and righteousness which man cannot explain.[2] Just because ($\gamma\acute{\alpha}\rho$ verse 18) God must feel anger against the whole world, not only the Gentiles, but also the Jews, and indeed every individual (chapter ii), therefore he bestows righteousness $\acute{\epsilon}\kappa$ $\pi\acute{\iota}\sigma\tau\epsilon\omega\varsigma$ $\epsilon\acute{\iota}\varsigma$ $\pi\acute{\iota}\sigma\tau\iota\nu$ (i.17, iii.21 ff.) and proves himself to be the just judge in his recognition of this righteousness (iii.26).

But this produces a fresh problem: If God is angry with those who do not pursue the way of faith, is this just? This problem is only one of the many in the continuous dialectic of the Bible which cannot be solved by reason. Everything is established according to God's will and plan, and yet this does not diminish the guilt of everything opposed to God, and therefore the wrath of God provoked by it is righteous without any qualification. There is only one refuge from this conclusion: Christ and faith in him (cf. p. 130).

---

[1] cf. Althaus, op. cit. (p. 84, n. 2), II, p. 163.
[2] cf. Schrenk, pp. 14 ff.

iii. *The manifestation of divine wrath*

(a) *In the portrayal and message of Jesus*

Wrath is an integrating feature in the gospel's picture of Jesus.[1] It is true that it is only seldom mentioned *expressis verbis* (ὀργή in Mark iii.5; ὀργίζομαι Mark i.41 (in a variant reading); cf. ἐμβριμάομαι in Matt. ix.30; Mark i.43; John xi.33, 38), but the fact itself appears more often.

That Jesus felt anger is firstly a sign that he was a human being of flesh and blood.[2] Yet it is never a merely human anger; it always implies something of the manner of God's anger. This is seen above all in those things at which and because of which Jesus is angry. His anger is aroused by hostility to God shown by various forms of powers and forces under the control of a will: he addresses Satan imperiously (Matt. iv.10, xvi.23)[3]; he censures the demons wrathfully (ἐπιτιμάω) in Mark i.25, ix.25; Luke iv.41); he confronts with

---

[1] cf. J. Ninck, *Jesus als Charakter* (1925), pp. 22-23; P. Feine, *Jesus* (1930), pp. 245 f.

[2] He does not resemble the Stoic with his 'inhuman' (cf. Sen. *Ep.* 99, k5: *inhumanitas, non virtus*) ἀταραξία (*impassiveness*). So there is nothing artificial when he becomes angry, as some have wished to deduce from the reflexive phrase ἐτάραξεν ἑαυτόν John xi.33; cf. Aug. in *Joh. Ev. Tract.* 49, 18; W. Heitmüller in *Die Schriften der NT ad loc.;* W. Bauer, *Kommentar z. Johannisev.* (²1925) *ad loc.*; H. J. Holtzmann, *Lehrbüch der neutestamentlichen Theologie* II (²1911), p. 193, n. 1; cf. R. Bultmann, *Johannisev.* (1941), p. 310, n. 4 and especially the completely misleading exegesis of the passage by H. J. Holtzmann, in *Handkommentar zum NT* IV (³1908) *ad loc.* The phrase means no more than the reading of the Western text, given also in P⁴⁵: ἐταράχθη τῷ πνεύματι (also xiii.21) ὡς ἐμβριμούμενος, that is to say, an intense and direct personal reaction (for its cause, cf. p. 94 and n. 1). On the other hand τῷ πνεύματι with ἐμβριμᾶσθαι, or with ταράττεσθαι can probably be taken with T. Zahn, *Johannisev.* (⁴1912), *ad loc.* to be so pregnant with meaning, as though it expressed that fact in Jesus God himself was roused to anger.

[3] Jesus regards Peter as actually a tool of Satan who conceals himself in him; cf. Stählin, *Skandalon* (1936), pp. 162 f.

bitter anger (ὀργισθείς)[1] the terrible disease of leprosy
(Mark i.41), he is deeply shocked by the diabolical
behaviour of men (John viii.44), especially of the
Pharisees (as πονηροὶ ὄντες in Matt. xii.34, as the mur-
derers of God's messengers in xxiii.33, as untruthful
hypocrites xv.7 *et passim*). This is the wrath of the Lord
of creation who is roused to indignation by those who
indignantly spurn him. Furthermore he is incensed
(ἐμβριμάομαι) against those whom he has healed and
whose disobedience he foresees[2] (Mark i.43[3]; Matt.
ix.39); and against the disciples and their lack of faith

---

[1] The reading, ὀργισθείς of D, it. (a, ff[2], r) Tat. is to be preferred
to the usual σπλαγχνισθείς which is more easily accounted for
(perhaps the origin of the one or the other is to be explained by
the confusion of the gutturals (in an Aramaic original: 'trḥm-
'tr'm); cf. E. Nestle, *Philologica sacra* (1896), p. 26; R. Harris,
'Artificial variants of the Text of the NT', Exp. 24 (1922), pp. 259-
261; so also J. Schniewind, *Markus* (NTD) *ad loc.* Ὀργίζεσθαι
denotes Jesus' 'embittered' grappling with the death-like disease,
and is thus equivalent to ἐμβριμᾶσθαι in John xi.33, 38 and
στενάζειν in Mark vii.34. It is very much less likely that Jesus is
indignant with the leper because he approached him contrary to
the law (cf. J. Weiss in *Die Schriften der NT* on Mark i.41) or because
he said doubtfully *if thou wilt* (Ephraem. *Evangelii concordantis
expositio*, translated by J. B. Aucher [1876], p. 144), or that the
anger had originally been attributed to the leper (change of
subject after ἥψατο, thus K. Lake, "Ἐμβριμησάμενος and ὀργισθείς
in Mark i.40-43', HThR 16 (1923), pp. 197 f.).

[2] We might also reflect that Jesus would be angry because he
foresees that many will be tempted to have a superficial faith due
to the miracles wrought on those who were healed.

[3] It is natural to attempt the reconstruction of an inner link
between the ὀργίζεσθαι before and the ἐμβριμᾶσθαι after the healing
of the leper, perhaps by referring to the unprecedented emotional
expenditure of power which appears in the θέλω (verse 41) and in
the ἐξέβαλεν (verse 43). But these are considerations scarcely
applicable to Jesus (cf. above and notes 1 and 2). On the other hand
the ἐμβριμησάμενος of verse 43 cannot be excised because it does not
fit into the theory of prophetic frenzy (which can occur only before

(xvii.17). He is distressed at the unbelieving Jews who give way in his presence to unrestrained grief although he has just acknowledged that he is the resurrection and the life (John xi.32), and immediately afterwards he is once more provoked by the spiteful remarks arising from their lack of faith and understanding (verse 38).[1] This is the wrath of the Lord to whom lack of faith and disobedience are affronts to his majesty. Above all Jesus is filled with sorrow mingled with wrath (μετ' ὀργῆς συλλυπούμενος in Mark iii.5)[2] at the Pharisees. It has no doubt a twofold cause: first the wrath of the merciful one towards the legal-minded who will not accept mercy as the new way of salvation, and who therefore allow themselves to be driven to mercilessness and actually to deadly enmity (verse 6).[3] It is at the same time the wrath of love which seeks to win the

the cure); thus C. Bonner, 'Traces of Thaumaturgic technique in the miracles', HThR 20 (1927), pp. 178-181) who regards ἐμβριμησάμενος as the original reading in verse 41; this would then have become *iratus* in the Itala and by retranslation ὀργισθείς in D.

[1] There has been much discussion concerning the reason for Jesus' distress in the story of Lazarus; for the various conjectures see F. Godet, *Commentar zu dem Ev. Joh.* (³1890), p. 401; H. J. Holtzmann, *op. cit.* (cf. p. 92, n. 2) *ad loc.*, Bauer, *ad loc.*; Bultmann *ad loc.* who explains ἐμβριμάομαι (like ταράσσω and στενάζω) as the *vox mystica* for the spiritual perturbation of a θεῖος ἄνθρω πος (in dependence on Bonner, *op. cit.* [p. 93, n. 3], pp. 176 ff.). Probably the most natural explanation is wrath on account of lack of faith, because Jesus' distress is mentioned both times obviously in connection with the behaviour of the Jews.

[2] cf. Schlatter, *Mark. ad loc.* In the parallels the reference to Jesus' ὀργή and λύπη is lacking. On the other hand an analogous association of grief and anger occurs in Jos. *Ant.* 16, 200.

[3] An astonishing parallel to the relationship of the Pharisees to Jesus is that of the Romans to Caesar whom they will not accept and finally kill, just because he is *lenissimus* (cf. his own declaration in Cic. *Att.* 9, 7 C 1, as well as *pro sua humanitate, indulgentia*, etc., cf. *ib.* A 2; further Sen. *De Clementia*). They do not want the new way of kindness and reconciliation, as Caesar himself emphasises

Pharisees too for the kingdom of mercy and to which they respond with hatred because they desire not mercy but law. So divine compassion[1] for their piety which is so remote from God is combined with holy wrath. It is the same wrath which Jesus illustrates in the parable of the master of the house (Luke xiv.21: τότε ὀργισθεὶς ὁ οἰκοδεσπότης) whose generous invitation is spurned by those who had received it. But an incomparably graver wrath is described in the case of the wicked servant (Matt. xviii.34: καὶ ὀργισθεὶς ὁ κύριος αὐτοῦ) whose reply to the boundless mercy shown to him was an incomprehensible lack of mercy.[2] In all these cases it is the holy wrath of rejected mercy and wounded love which is discharging itself. Lastly, Jesus is filled with terrible wrath for the towns which had refused to listen to the call for repentance (Matt. xi.20 ff.) and for the traders in the temple who by dishonouring the house of God showed that they did not take God himself seriously (Matt. xxi.12 ff.; cf. John ii.13 ff.),[3] and in a symbolic act which is strange to the modern reader[4] he

energetically. Cf. now E. Stauffer, 'Clementia Caesaris' in *Schrift und Bekenntnis, Zeugnisse lutherischer Theologie* (1950), pp. 174-184, especially pp. 182 f.

[1] This is indicated by the compound συλλυπέομαι, cf. Pr.-Bauer *sv*, etc.

[2] The Baptist still keeps the door open for the Pharisees (cf. Matt. iii.8) and Jesus himself does so even more; his divine love sorrows for each one who is lost (cf. Luke xix.41 ff.; perhaps also John xi.38) and maintains to the end the promise of salvation to the Pharisees as well (cf. Luke xiii.35). On the other hand the disciple who has been forgiven but refuses forgiveness suffers final condemnation of wrath; the reason for this judgement in Matt. xviii.34 is the same as that in Heb. vi.4-6.

[3] Here the φραγέλλιον in verse 15 is both the symbol and the weapon of the divine wrath, announced already by the prophets for the cult which had become completely externalised.

[4] When Jesus cursed the fig-tree in anger, the question as to whether his anger was just is raised in regard to him too; for the time when figs ripened was long past (cf. the commentaries). This

reveals his wrath for those who withhold from him the fruits of repentance (Mark xi.14; cf. Luke xiii.7). This is the wrath of the eschatological judge who has authority to destroy, to exclude from the community of God (ἐκβάλλω in Matt. xxi.12; cf. xxii.13, xxv.30; Luke xiii.28), to thrust down into Hades (Matt. xi.23), and who is already exercising this authority.

It can be seen from what has just been said that Jesus was conscious of the fact, and often demonstrated it in his sayings and parables, that when his anger is provoked, it is fundamentaly already the manifestation of the eschatological wrath of God. It is one trait in the rich picture of the last things fulfilled in Jesus' coming. It is he who is the enraged Lord of the Last Judgement (cf. Ps. ii.12),[1] he who refuses all knowledge of those against whom his wrath is aroused (Matt. vii.23, xxv.12, Luke xiii.27),[2] he who destroys his enemies in his rage (Luke xix.27, xii.46 and parallels; cf. Matt. xxii.7, and allows those who are rejected to be thrown εἰς τὴν κάμινον τοῦ πυρός (Matt. xiii.42; cf. verse 49 f., xxv.41) and εἰς τὸ σκότος τὸ ἐξώτερον (xxii.3, xxv.30), or into imprisonment for debt without hope of release (xviii.34). This must be mentioned here although the key-word ὀργίζομαι is used only twice in the passages referred to (Matt. xviii.34, xxii.7). It needs all the more emphasis since, with a correspondence to the

is probably one of the many traits in Jesus' parables and symbolic acts which shock us and the only purpose of which is to direct our attention to what is described and to emphasise its real importance.

[1] On the other hand it is worth noticing that in Luke xiii.9 Jesus says ἐκκόψεις (*you can cut it down*), not ἐκκόψω (*I will cut it down*). When judgement is passed in the historical era the parts to be played by the wrathful judge and the merciful intercessor are divided between the Father and the Son.

[2] The sevenfold 'woes' in Matt. xxiii expresses something similar; with this word Jesus as the judge at the present time pronounces God's sentence of wrath.

opening sections of the New Testament, the last book takes up again with its characteristic intensity and vividness the picture of the wrathful king and judge of the last days. Thus, for example, there is the picture in Rev. xix.15 which presents the King of Kings and Lord of Lords himself treading the winepress of the wrath of God the Almighty in a garment drenched with blood and with a sword issuing out of his mouth (cf. pp. 102, 115), and again the particularly striking phrase of the ὀργὴ τοῦ ἀρνίου in Rev. vi.16[1] (cf. also xiv.10). In the case of this apparently impossible mixture of images, we must consider firstly that ἀρνίον (in contrast to ἀμνός in John i.29, etc.) is also associated with the image of a strong young ram; secondly, and above all, that it is the same Christ who, defenceless as a lamb, had once to submit to the judgement of men, but who will then himself as a wrathful judge pass judgement on men with terror (cf. especially Rev. xix.11 ff.). His wrath will come in the first instance upon those who scorn the 'lamb's' offering of himself.

(b)   At work in history and at the end of time

Like many other NT concepts and important ideas— βασιλεία, δικαιοσύνη,[2] σωτηρία—ὀργή is a concept which

---

[1] The authenticity of the phrase καὶ ἀπὸ τῆς ὀργῆς αὐτοῦ has been challenged (E. Vischer, *Die Offenbarung Joh.* (1881), pp. 40 f.; F. Spitta, *Die Offenbarung des Joh.* (1889), pp. 27 f.; J. Weiss in *Schr. NT* on Rev. vi.16; E. Sievers, 'Die Johannesapokalypse klanglich untersucht und herausgegeben', ASG 38, 1 (1925), p. 31, etc. So also Procksch in the first form of this article on Wrath. This view is maintained firstly because the phrase is tagged on to the end of the phrase ἀπὸ προσώπου τοῦ καθημένου ἐπὶ τοῦ θρόνου, secondly because in verse 17 the majority of the witnesses read αὐτοῦ instead of αὐτῶν. Nevertheless a later interpolation of the phrase seems to me improbable; Christ is at once both saviour and Judge—the words *wrath of the lamb* express this in terse impressiveness and the day of judgement is the day of *his* (αὐτοῦ) wrath in verse 17.

[2] cf. *Basileia* (1957) and *Righteousness* (1951) in this series.

can possess both a decidedly eschatological character and a decidedly contemporary one.[1] As in the case of those central ideas, ὀργή applied to contemporary situations assumes a different and provisional quality in comparison with its eschatological counterpart. Both of these descriptions are of about equal importance in the NT, if not numerically, yet in actual fact.

(i) Eschatological wrath is distinguished by some typical adjuncts, antitheses and metaphors. The following eschatological technical terms occur in connection with ὀργή: the verbs ἔρχομαι (I Thess. i.10; cf. Eph. v.6; Rev. xi.18) and μέλλω (Matt. iii.7), especially their present participles (cf TWNT II, pp. 666 ff.), also σώζω (Rom. v.9) and ἀποκαλύπτω (Rom. i.18; cf. TWNT III, p. 586; but cf. p. 101, n. 1), and in particular ἡμέρα as the designation coined by the prophets for the day of Yahweh[2] (e.g. Zeph. i.15; cf. Ps. cx (LXX, cix), 5 et passim, cf. pp. 34 f., 71 but also p. 42), which reappears in the Pseudepigrapha (e.g. Jub. xxiv.28, 30) and in the Talmud (B.AZ, 18b; B. BB, 10a; cf. p. 110 n. 2), and is also taken up into the NT (Rom. ii.5; Rev. xi.17). The following antitheses to the eschatological ὀργή occur: ζωὴ αἰώνιος (Rom. ii.7; cf. verse 5) and περιποίησις σωτηρίας (I Thess. v.9). Amongst the

---

[1] cf. L. Pinoma, 'Der Zorn Gottes', ZSTh 17 (1940), p. 590. Ritschl, *Rechtfertigung und Versöhnung*, p. 153, thought he could prove that the conception of God's wrath in the NT is only applied eschatologically and is no longer (as in the OT [pp. 33 ff.] and in Judaism [pp. 66 f.]) used in judging contemporary phenomena and that thereby he demonstrated that it is no longer binding for the Christian faith. But this kind of consistently eschatological interpretation is also one-sided and leads to wrong conclusions (cf. F. Weber, *passim*; Cr.-Kö. pp. 813-816; P. Feine, p. 207; R. Bultmann, *Johannisev.*, p. 121, n. 4).

[2] Occasionally in the OT ἡμέρα ὀργῆς is also used for historical disasters; cf. II Kings xix.3 and in the parallel text in Isa. xxxvii.3; probably also in Job xx.28, xxi.30.

images for divine wrath (cf. pp. 108 ff.) those of fire (Matt. iii.10-12), of the cup (Rev. xiv.10) and of the winepress (xix.15) bear an eschatological stamp.

The significance of eschatological wrath for the NT message is demonstrated most clearly by the fact that the NT, following directly in the wake of the OT prophets (cf. p. 34), starts with the announcement of the ὀργὴ μέλλουσα (Matt. iii.7) and ends on the same theme (Rev. up to chapter xix). John the Baptist, with his preaching of the coming wrath of God[1] (Matt. iii.7, 10-12) and with his baptism which aims at deliverance from it (cf. pp. 111, 129), provides the prelude and in this matter Jesus followed him. Jesus seldom speaks *expressis verbis* of divine wrath (cf. p. 92); the noun ὀργή occurs in one passage alone, in the Lucan form of the discourse concerning the future (xxi.23), and the verb ὀργίζομαι is found in this eschatological sense only a few times in parables (in Matt. xxii.7; somewhat differently in Luke xiv.21; cf. also Matt. xviii.34). But the thing itself is a unifying feature in Jesus' picture of the future, just as it is in that of his apostles, particularly in that of Paul and of the seer John (cf. p. 100). In fact there are two points in the picture of the future at which the eschatological ὀργή has its appropriate place, i.e. in the period of distress before the end and in the distress during the judgement at the end itself.

Jesus' only statement containing the word ὀργή (Luke xxi.23) occurs in the description of the messianic woes, where it is almost synonymous with ἀνάγκη,[2] and where in the synoptic parallels (Matt. xxiv.21; Mark xiii.19) θλῖψις is found. These are all technical terms for the

---

[1] According to the account of the evangelist John not only the first words of John the Baptist, but also his last ones (iii.36), dealt with the wrath of God.

[2] cf. for this close association of *ira deum* and *fatum* amongst the Romans, e.g. Tac. *Hist.* IV 26. Cf. p. 11.

eschatological distress, the chief event of which is the destruction of Jerusalem (cf. verses 21, 24). We are therefore concerned here with an activity of ὀργή in historical times, and consequently with one of limited duration, verse 24: ἄχρι οὗ πληρωθῶσιν καιροὶ ἐθνῶν.

The Rabbis already used 'wrath' occasionally as a designation for the judgement of Gehenna itself.[1] Similarly in Paul's writings ὀργή can have the same meaning as ἀποκάλυψις δικαιοκρισίας τοῦ θεοῦ (Rom. ii.5) and in Revelation as καιρὸς τῶν νεκρῶν κριθῆναι (xi.18). Clearly ὀργή here is not so much the righteous wrath of the judge of the world himself as that which he inflicts (cf. p. 87), the ἐκδίκησις (cf. Luke xxi.22 f.), the opposite of δικαίωσις that is to say the 'refusal of salvation'.[2] Therefore the last day is named from its most salient feature ἡμέρα ὀργῆς (Rom. ii.5; Rev. vi.17). The fact that in the first place where ὀργή appears in Revelation we read: ἦλθεν ἡ ἡμέρα ἡ μεγάλη τῆς ὀργῆς shows that the whole drama of wrath in the Revelation takes place on this one 'day' of judgement. In a succession of ever fresh calamities wrath is poured out: when the sixth seal is broken (vi.12 ff.); when the last trumpet is sounded (xi.18); when each of the seven bowls of wrath is poured out (xv f.); when judgement is pronounced over Babylon (xvi.19), and at the parousia of the Lord and Judge who himself treads the winepress of his wrath (xix.15).

(ii) In the NT wrathful condemnation at the present time is found in a varied relationship to the eschatological judgement of wrath. We have already seen (pp. 95 f.) how the Jesus of the gospels, when provoked to anger in this world, appears already as the person in whom the messiah and judge of the last days, indeed the holy God himself, is present. Further, Jesus displays

---

[1] cf. Str.-B. I, pp. 115 f. Cf. p. 110, n. 2.
[2] Cr. Kö. p. 814.

in different ways in his discourses wrath in action in history (e.g. in Luke xiii.2 ff.). Paul too speaks plainly in several contexts about the effect of God's wrath in this era. The first passage to be named here is Rom. i.18: ἀποκαλύπτεται γὰρ ὀργὴ θεοῦ ἀπ' οὐρανοῦ ἐπὶ πᾶσαν ἀσέβειαν καὶ ἀδικίαν ἀνθρώπων τῶν τὴν ἀλήθειαν ἐν ἀδικίᾳ κατεχόντων. There can hardly be any doubt that this is an announcement of a contemporary manifestation of God's wrath.[1] It is manifested at the same time in every detail in a manner analogous[2] to the δικαιοσύνη θεοῦ. Moreover the two manifestations are connected by a significant γάρ. The fact that apart from πίστις there is only ὀργή for all mankind (cf. iii.9 ff., 23) is the indispensable presupposition of δικαιοσύνη being manifested only ἐκ πίστεως.[3] The significance of the γάρ is the same as that of the double γάρ in iii.22 f. or of the ἵνα in Gal. iii.22. But the twofold manifestation of God's wrath and righteousness depends exclusively on Christ; since the time when he came into the world the eschatological judgement of the world is taking place, the acquittal (justification) as well as the condemnation in wrath.[4] For the term ἀποκαλύπτω stamps the message as an eschatological act of salvation.[5] At the same time ἀποκαλύπτω indicates in both cases a veiled manifestation,

[1] The present tense must be taken neither as bringing the future vividly into the present nor as the gnomic present of a doctrine of things to come, derived from prophecy (thus Ritschl, *Rechtfertigung und Versöhnung*, pp. 142-147), as is certainly the case in I Cor. iii.13 (ἡ ἡμέρα . . . ἐν πυρὶ ἀποκαλύπτεται); since this interpretation is excluded in the case of i.17, it must be rejected also for the verse immediately following (Cr. Kö. p. 815).

[2] cf. especially A. Schlatter, *Römerbrief*, p. 46 and for the dialectic of the relationship of the two manifestations W. Elert, *Der Christliche Glaube* (1940), pp. 170-176.

[3] cf. A. Schlatter, *Römerbrief*, p. 52; cf. p. 91.

[4] cf. the contemporary judgement in John and on this G. Stählin, 'Zum Problem der johanneischen Eschatologie', ZNW 33 (1934), p. 238; Cr. Kö. pp. 814 f.   [5] Bornkamm, p. 239.

8

i.e. one that is manifested only to the believer. This applies just as strictly to the ἀποκάλυψις ὀργῆς as to the ἀποκάλυψις δικαιοσύνης. Admittedly the ἐν αὐτῷ in Rom. i.17 is not to be linked formally with i.18; but only in the sphere of the gospel is it manifest that the abysmal sinfulness of the world is a manifestation of divine wrath.[1] Yet every such veiled manifestation in time points to a complete manifestation at the end. Hence beside the proclamation of the present manifestation of wrath there stands necessarily that of the future wrath (ii.8), just as the message of the present justification (iii.24, 28) is accompanied by a promise of it in the future (verse 30).

Corresponding to this, in the other case in which Paul speaks of the ὀργή (θεοῦ), beside the eschatological factor a contemporary one can usually be identified (thus in Rom. ii.5, 8, ix.22). Contrariwise where wrath in action at the present time is mentioned (as in Rom. iii.5, iv.15, xiii.4 f.; I Thess. ii.16), the eschatological aspect is never completely lacking.[2] In Rom. iii.7 τί ἔτι κἀγὼ ὡς ἁμαρτωλὸς κρίνομαι is parallel with μὴ ἄδικος ὁ θεὸς ὁ ἐπιφέρων τὴν ὀργήν; in verse 5. The present ἐπιφέρων points back to the manifestation of God's wrath in the present in i.18 f.; but κρίνομαι, likewise in the present tense but undoubtedly eschatological, does lend to ὀργή the quality of eschatological wrath.[3]

---

[1] Bultmann, p. 271, ET p. 275; Elert, *op. cit.* (see p. 101, n. 2).

[2] The case is different in Heb. iii.11, iv.3. Here in the quotation from Ps. xcv.11 it is the completely uneschatological divine wrath of the OT which from time to time raged over Israel and the pagan nations.

[3] Wetter, p. 29 explains Paul's argument as follows: if God is already the future judge of the world (verse 6), his present exercise of authority as judge is certainly also just, that is to say, a conclusion *a maiori ad minus*. But the present and future operations of his wrath cannot be divided up in this way; cf. T. Zahn, *Römerbrief* (1910), *ad loc.*

(iii) A striking postponement of the judgement of wrath is noticeable in the NT. God himself appears to observe the rule required of men: ἔστω πᾶς ἄνθρωπος . . . βραδὺς εἰς ὀργήν in James i.19. This explains why so often we cannot see any effect of his wrath where it would be most expected.

The theme of wrath's delay is found in a variety of modifications already before the NT; amongst the Greeks (Homer, Solon, cf. pp. 4 f.), in the OT, particularly in the form of the vivid expression 'erek 'appaim (=μακρόθυμος etc., cf. TWNT IV, p. 378; cf. p. 14, n. 2; pp. 42, 80),[1] and in Judaism (e.g. Syr. Bar. lix.6). Here it is admittedly constricted by particularism to serve either as a one-sided means for the salvation of Israel (e.g. J. Taan. 2, 65b, 44 ff.; especially 50-58[2]), or as an expression of θυμός against the nations (e.g. II Macc. vi.14). Both are combined in B. Erub. 22a: *slow to wrath against the righteous, slow to wrath against the wicked*.[3]

In the NT the idea of delayed wrath forms the background to three passages in the letter to the Romans,[4] and in two of them a double effect can be observed,

[1] In addition, cf. Jer. li.33 (*yet a little while* denotes the period of time which the wrath of God allows itself before it breaks out into judgement [= harvest]), perhaps also in Nahum i.2 f.

[2] 'erek 'appaim (in Joel ii.13) is understood here in the sense of *keeping wrath at a distance* and explained by the conception of wrath personified as two angels of destruction—two owing to the dual 'appaim—, 'wrath' and 'resentment', ordered to go far away. Thus Israel is able to repent during the long period until they approach from the distance (cf. Str. B. III, p. 30).

[3] Here the dual is explained as two faces of God, the one friendly, the other resentful (L. Goldschmidt, *Der babylonische Talmud* II (1930), p. 69, n. 132).

[4] It can also be found in some of Jesus' parables: e.g. in Matt. xiii.24 ff. the postponement of the judgement serves to preserve the δίκαιοι; in Luke xiii.8 it affords an opportunity for the fruits of repentance.

similar to that in the rabbinic sayings. In Rom. ix.22 (cf. pp. 88 f., 108 f.) the postponement of the judgement of wrath serves on the one hand to demonstrate all the more powerfully the might of God's anger against the σκεύη ὀργῆς, on the other hand an all the more glorious manifestation of his compassion for the σκεύη ἐλέους. In Rom. ii.4 we see clearly how the twofold function of postponing God's wrath (ἀνοχὴ καὶ μακροθυμία) can take effect not only in different people, but in one and the same person. It can lead to μετάνοια and thereby to δικαιοσύνη ἐκ πίστεως and thus also to the ἔργον ἀγαθόν. On the other hand it can lead to an accumulation of the store of wrath until in the ἡμέρα ὀργῆς καὶ ἀποκαλύψεως δικαιοκρισίας τοῦ θεοῦ the time arrives when the payment of the whole large sum is required (cf. pp. 115f.). Lastly in Rom. xii.19 man is urged, by practising retribution on himself, to seek to forestall the divine wrath whilst it delays (but cf. p. 122, n. 1).

(iv) Thus a historical survey of the doctrine shows the following result. Salvation history is divided into two periods, one marked by ὀργή, the other by δικαιοσύνη θεοῦ. There are two αἰῶνες, οὗτος and ἐκεῖνος, which nevertheless overlap in the time of Christ between the two parousias. Therefore during this period the twofold manifestation of Rom. i.17 f. occurs simultaneously. The manifestation of wrath turns our eyes in two directions. It discloses the history of mankind as standing under ὀργή since the fall of man, and on the other hand precisely on that account, as being the anticipation of the world judgement. In fact it is like the tinder at which the ὀργή of the aeon of wrath is kindled, namely the law: ὁ νόμος ὀργὴν κατεργάζεται in Rom. iv.15. The law too, like the gospel, is a gift of God's love,[1] and as indifference to the goodness and forbearance of God

---

[1] Orthodox Jews to this day regard the law in this light.

in the gospel arouses ὀργή, so also does indifference to the law. This is not the purpose of the law[1]—it only looks like it to the transgressor. When God is provoked to anger by the law's infringement, that too is the reaction of neglected love which intended the law to be a benefit to men.[2]

(v) When eschatological events are anticipated in history, a transference takes place, as it were, from the instantaneous to the gradual. Events turn into conditions, the μέλλουσα ὀργή becomes the ὀργὴ μένουσα. In John iii.36 we read: ὁ ἀπειθῶν τῷ υἱῷ οὐκ ὄψεται ζωήν, ἀλλ᾽ ἡ ὀργὴ τοῦ θεοῦ μένει ἐπ᾽ αὐτόν. What does this mean? Does wrath remain until the end or to eternity? The second alternative would mean that in view of the present judgement of wrath the expectation of the future one is completely cancelled. But as John's views on eschatology are not exhausted by his picture of fulfilled eschatology,[3] the answer may be given here that the μένουσα ὀργή will be superseded by the μέλλουσα ὀργή.[4] But beyond this the question remains: is there in the view of the NT an eternal ὀργή?

The answer of the Greek world to this question is yes, that of the OT no. The myths for example of Sisyphus and of Prometheus tell of the eternal raging of the gods' μῆνις (*wrath*).[5] On the other hand the Lord of the Bible says: *I will not be angry for ever* (Jer. iii.12: cf. Ps. ciii.9 ff.,

---

[1] Nor is it an unalterable decree (cf. Wetter, p. 39, etc.). This is the somewhat one-sided view of Paul (cf. p. 126).

[2] cf. von Jüchen, pp. 33 ff. and above p. 39.

[3] cf. G. Stählin, *op. cit.* (p. 101, n. 4), pp. 253-257.

[4] So also Procksch; Cr. Kö. p. 814.

[5] Definitions of antiquity distinguished between θυμός and ὀργή as temporary and long-lasting (thus Pseudo-Ammonius, *De adfinium Vocabulorum Differentia sv*). But there is no suggestion here that ὀργή will last for ever. The same is true of analogous definitions in Diogenes Laertius VII 1, 63, Greg. Naz. *Carmina* II 34, 44, and Theodoret on Ps. lxviii (Masoretic text lxix), 25.

etc.).[1] Judaism occasionally mentions eternal wrath, thus in Sib. III.309 (conjecture of Geffcken): *and to the children of wrath eternal perdition,* and Jochanan ben Zakkai (B. Ber. 28b): *the king of kings whose wrath when he is provoked is an everlasting wrath.* But in this matter Jewish opinions are not unanimous; e.g. according to Sanh. 10, 6d the heat of divine wrath hangs over the world only so long as there are wicked men in it[2] and B. Ber. 7 dilates on the fact that God is indeed provoked to anger daily, but each time only for a fleeting moment.

In the NT itself there are passages which speak of a definite limit to the duration of wrath (thus Luke xxi.23, cf. p. 99) beside others which appear to reckon with an anger which burns eternally, as in Matt. iii.12: the πῦρ ἄσβεστον is here a metaphor for ὀργή (similarly in Mark ix.43 ff.); the same applies to the πῦρ αἰώνιον of Matt. xviii.8, xxv.41; Jude 7. In Matt. xviii.34 the wrath of the king vents itself upon the wicked servant in a manner implying eternal duration, for whilst in prison for debt when could he discharge his endless debt? Similarly the wine of wrath in Rev. xiv.10 (*et passim*) is obviously parallel to the torments in the sulphurous lake which last εἰς αἰῶνας αἰώνων (verse 11; xx.10). But in all the last named cases it is a question not of the wrath itself, but of the punishment inflicted by it, which according to the main line (cf. TWNT I, p. 390: ἀποκατάστασις) of NT statements is certainly of eternal duration. It is only in this sense that one can

[1] But cf. p. 44. See p. 107, n. 2 on the frequent mention of wrath εἰς τέλος in the OT.

[2] Occasionally the Rabbis also reckon in a theologically untenable manner on wrath coming to an end; thus in various comments on Ps. xcv.11 by means of which they apparently wish to avoid the conclusion of Heb. iv.3 ff.: Num. R. 14 (177c) in Str. B. III, p. 685; T. Sanh. 13, 10 f. (435) in Str. B. III, p. 409. Midr. Qoh. 10, 20 (49b) in Str. B. III, pp. 678.

speak of eternal ὀργή in the NT.[1] But God's wrath too, as such, is certainly something enduring, because it is not a quickly evaporating passion, but the holy repugnance to all that is not holy; it endures until the last will opposed to God is subdued (Rev. xx.10, 14, xxi.8). The question concerning the eternal duration of the ὀργὴ θεοῦ is posed directly in I Thess. ii.16 where it is said of the Jews: ἔφθασεν (or ἐφθακεν) ἐπ' αὐτοὺς ἡ ὀργὴ εἰς τέλος. What does εἰς τέλος mean? *Until the end* (and then no longer)[2] or *for ever?* It might mean: owing to the continuous serious transgressions of the Jews, God's wrath has been in operation again and again *until the last days which are now dawning.* But probably we have here merely the very ordinary and already somewhat hackneyed εἰς τέλος with which the LXX renders the Hebrew.[3] εἰς τέλος can certainly have the serious meaning of εἰς τὸν αἰῶνα, e.g. in Ps. ciii.9 [LXX, cii.9]: οὐκ εἰς τέλος ὀργισθήσεται οὐδὲ εἰς τὸν αἰῶνα μηνιεῖ, but probably I Thess. ii.16 does after all mean *for ever,* without any thought being given to what is involved in the eternal duration of this wrath.[4] Reflection might indeed suggest that, because the Jews had rejected Christ and deliverance in him from the ὀργὴ θεοῦ, they would be handed over to eternal wrath.[5] But in that

---

[1] cf. Althaus, *op. cit.* (p. 84, n. 2), II, p. 31.

[2] τέλος is perhaps used in the sense of annihilation, as in the parallel (is it the original of this passage? or is it derived from it?) in Test. Levi vi.11: *The wrath of the Lord came upon them* (i.e. the Shechemites) *to bring annihilation.* Annihilation causes wrath to cease as well.

[3] The frequent combination of εἰς τέλος with ἕως πότε, e.g. in Ps. lxxix.5 [LXX, lxxviii.5]: ἕως πότε, κύριε, ὀργισθήσῃ εἰς τέλος; shows that εἰς τέλος was used merely as a rhetorical expression. (Cf. also on *lānesaḥ,* D. Winton Thomas, JSS 1 (1956), pp. 106-109.)

[4] Thus for example in Jub. xxiv.28 (*cursed be the Philistines unto the day of wrath and indignation*) the thought of the end of the curse is of no importance. It means quite simply: *as long as the earth lasts, for ever.*   [5] Thus Pr.-Bauer *sv*; Dibelius, *Theologie ad. loc.*

case the passage would be in irreconcilable contradiction to Rom. xi where Paul expounds the principles of his eschatological views concerning the Jews. These principles may be regarded as determining the interpretation of other passages dealing with the Jews, such as I Thess. ii.14 ff. This 'anti-Semitic' section cannot therefore be accepted as authority for views of an ὀργή which lasts for ever.

iv. *The wrath of God in the imagery of the NT*

The statements in the NT concerning God's wrath are, like those in the OT (cf. pp. 29 f.) clothed to an extraordinary extent in metaphors. As in the case of other NT concepts, the images provide all kinds of indications to enable the ideas associated with these concepts to be more clearly grasped. This is true of the concept of ὀργή although many of these images have become trite figures of speech from having been used over and over again.

(*a*) Images of the man provoked to anger occur in some of Jesus' parables (Matt. xviii.34, xxii.7; cf. Luke xiv.21). In these the ὀργίζεσθαι of the king or the master always indicates the turning point in the story, and going beyond the story to the rejection of the Jews and all who go the same way. The same wrath of the judge, but without the actual words ὀργή or ὀργίζομαι appears in the parables of the fig-tree (Luke xiii.6 ff.; Mark xi.13 f.; cf. pp. 95 f.), as well as in the great picture of the judgement in Matt. xxv, which emphasises the wrath at the contempt of God, at actual affronts to him (verses 24, 26, 30), and at the complete lack of love (verses 41 ff.).

(*b*) Metaphors for those struck by wrath. The metaphor of σκεύη ὀργῆς in Rom. ix.22 (cf. p. 104) is derived from the LXX (Jer. l.25 [LXX, xxvii.25]) and occurs again in Symmachus (Isa. xiii.5). But corresponding to the breadth of meaning of its Hebrew equivalent *kᵉlē*, σκεῦος (ὀργῆς) in the Greek OT means the instrument with which, or rather in the NT that on which, God's wrath operates. In the former they are weapons out of God's arsenal of wrath (Jer. l.25 [LXX, xxvii.25]) or soldiers in God's army at the world judgement (Isa. xiii.5). In the latter they are the vessels into which God's wrath is, so to speak, poured so as completely to fill up their destiny of being devoted to destruction.[1] The counterpart is the σκεύη ἐλέους which are similarly filled with compassion. Yet a change in the contents is possible before the τέλος which brings about the final dispensation of the ὀργή when Christians experience in themselves that from being τέκνα φύσει ὀργῆς they become τέκνα θεοῦ (Eph. ii.3), and vice versa when the wicked servant doubtless from being a σκεῦος ἐλέους becomes a σκεῦος ὀργῆς, or when the Jews from being υἱοὶ τῆς βασιλείας (Matt. viii.12) become υἱοὶ γεέννης (xxiii.15).[2]

The phrase τέκνα ὀργῆς in Eph. ii.3 similarly has some pre-NT prototypes.[3] It belongs to the large group

[1] For this distinction between the meanings of σκεύη ὀργῆς, cf. von Hofmann, op. cit. (p. 90, n. 1). A different view is held by T. Zahn, Römerbrief (1910), ad loc. who will accept here too only the meaning of instrument. But there is no doubt that the image of the potter naturally first suggests vessels. Yet it is correct that the meaning of σκεῦος passes imperceptibly from the active meaning of σκεῦος εἰς τιμήν (verse 21; cf. II Tim. ii.20) = utensil, vessel for an honourable purpose—to the passive one. Thus a vessel out of which the wrathful judgement of God is poured out over others, such as Pharaoh, is after all itself permanently suffering from the effects of this wrath and in particular is itself destined for the endless judgement of wrath.

[2] Similarly Elert, op. cit. (p. 101, n. 2) p. 563: ' "Children of wrath" too, who are probably none other than the "vessels of wrath", can be promoted in Christ Jesus into the heavenly nature (Eph. ii. 3-6).'

[3] Apoc. Mos. iii (Tischendorf, p. 2): Cain = ὀργῆς υἱός; Sib. III.309 (cf. p. 106): καὶ θυμοῦ τέκνοις αἰώνιος 'ἐξολόθρευσις,

of words denoting close relationship with τέκνον or υἱός (so that there can no longer be a question of any imagery). The imperfect ἤμεθα τέκνα φύσει ὀργῆς means: although φύσις seems to express the original, the natural condition of lying under the judgement of wrath (cf. Gal. ii.15; Rom. xi.21, 24), yet it has become a matter of the past, it has been replaced by a new ζωοποίησις, by another 'φύσις'; for in the sight of God there is, as it were, a change of family (John i.12; Matt. xxiii.15) through adoption, a fresh υἱοθεσία, and thus also a change of φύσις (cf. Rom. vi.5).[1]

(c) The images or wrath itself are taken mainly from three spheres:

(i) The image of fire (πῦρ)—used originally for the passionate outburst of wrath (cf. pp. 14, 30), then for the judgement of wrath—combines several conceptions: an image of the terrors and torments at the end, a conception of the final judgement itself (e.g. I Cor. iii.13, 15) and that of the 'fires of hell' (Matt. v.22, xviii.9), of the πῦρ αἰώνιον (Matt. xviii.8, xxv.41; Jude 7). This is the threefold background to the threefold image of fire with which the Baptist in Matt. iii.10-12 develops his saying concerning the μέλλουσα ὀργή (verse 7).[2] Closely connected with this there is in Matt. iii.10

i.e. *for the children of Babylon there comes eternal perdition.* T. Zahn, *Römerbrief* (1910), p. 457, n. 22 compares also the completely literal statement ἀνὴρ ἐπιθυμιῶν (*longed for*) in Dan. x.11 (Theodotion).

[1] σύμφυτος *like by nature, kindred* (Plat. *Phileb.* 16c), *conformed* (= συμμορφιζόμενος in Phil. iii.10), as happened in the case of Stephen, the prototype (Acts vi.15, vii.59 f.). If a man receives a share in Jesus' mortal body, he will also have a share in the body of his resurrection (cf. Rom. viii.29; Phil. iii.21; cf. TWNT V, p. 192). This exegesis of σύμφυτος must at least be considered beside the usual one of *grown together.*

[2] Verse 9 disturbs the continuity and probably did not belong here originally. On the other hand verse 8 forms the presupposition of verse 10 which with ἤδη is directly linked with the μέλλουσα

and parallels the saying about the axe. This is another image for the impending divine wrath. Whilst Matt. iii.10 refers to the eschatological wrath, Luke xiii.7 (Codex Bezae, cf. verse 9) applies to the historical situation (cf. p. 96 n. 1).

(ii) In the Baptist's preaching, as already occasionally in the OT, the image of water-floods (cf. Job xl.11) is mingled with that of fire (cf. Ezek. xxi.31 [Heb. 36]; xxii.31; cf. p. 31). This combination of the images is suggested by the twofold tradition of the flood and of the rain of fire on Sodom and Gomorrah, as well as by the expectation, corresponding to the fundamental biblical conception of the similarity of the primeval and the final days,[1] that at the end there will be a great universal fire and also a great universal flood.[2] This connection is the result of observing that the Baptist links not only the image of baptism by fire, but also his baptism by water with the $\mu\acute{\epsilon}\lambda\lambda ο\upsilon\sigma\alpha$ $\dot{ο}ρ\gamma\acute{\eta}$ (Matt. iii.7). Water shares with fire—as 'beneficent' as it is 'terrible' —and other elemental forces,[3] an ambivalent nature; it can be death-bringing or life-giving.[4] This is the basis

$\dot{ο}ρ\gamma\acute{\eta}$ of verse 7. How closely wrath and fire were seen to be associated already in Judaism is shown by the rabbinic sayings in which '(day of) wrath' is regularly interpreted as hell-fire; cf. B. AZ 18; B. BB 10 and on these note 360 in Goldschmidt (p. 103, n. 3), VIII, p. 38; also B. Ned. 22a (Goldschmidt V, p. 410). For the baptism of fire, cf. C. M. Edsman, *Le Baptême de feu* (1940).

[1] cf. H. Gunkel, *Schöpfung und Chaos in Urzeit und Endzeit* ([2]1921).

[2] cf. Vit. Ad. xlix. A contradiction between the expectation of an eschatological flood and of the promise of Gen. ix.11 appears only if the emphasis on the phrase 'never again all' is ignored. For a part of mankind will be saved from the final flood. cf. R. Eisler, $'I\eta\sigma ο\hat{\upsilon}ς$ $\beta\alpha\sigma\iota\lambda\epsilon\grave{\upsilon}ς$ $ο\grave{\upsilon}$ $\beta\alpha\sigma\iota\lambda\epsilon\acute{\upsilon}\sigma\alpha ς$ (II, 1933), pp. 101 ff.

[3] cf. the opposite effects in the case of $\dot{ο}\sigma\mu\acute{\eta}$ (II Cor. ii.16), $\lambda\acute{\iota}\theta ο ς$ (Luke xx.17 f.), etc.

[4] Their interchangeability is the salient point in the Adapa myth (AOT ed. 1, pp. 36 f.; ANET, pp. 101 ff. Cf. *Chant de la Saussaye* I, p. 600; K. Galling, article on Water in RGG[2] V, 1770 f.).

of the fact—and not only the rite of immersion—that baptism can be already for Jesus the symbol of death, and indeed of his own death (Mark x.38; Luke xii.50).[1] By contrast, the meaning of salvation arises from the conception of the water of life as well as from the act of emerging, typifying the resurrection or new birth. Baptism is one of the numerous symbolic actions of the gospel which are not only ambiguous, but which often have in fact two or more meanings. Already for John the Baptist it is clearly just as much a symbol pointing forward to baptism of the spirit, as it is a preliminary image anticipating the judgement of annihilation at the end.[2] In the first sense it awards the gift of salvation of the last days ($\epsilon\grave{\iota}s$ $\check{\alpha}\phi\epsilon\sigma\iota\nu$ $\grave{\alpha}\mu\alpha\rho\tau\iota\hat{\omega}\nu$ in Mark i.4; cf. Acts ii.28 where in the same way baptism, forgiveness and the gift of the spirit are linked together). In the second sense it procures deliverance from the baptism of fire[3] of the last judgement. Therefore whoever desires baptism, hopes to escape from the future wrath (Matt. iii.7). Yet that on which from the beginning the power

[1] This conception, which occurs both in the Marcan tradition and in the material peculiar to Luke, no doubt belongs to the basic stock of Jesus' sayings. Like the logion about the ransom, it must not be prised by critical manipulation out of the original core of the Jesus-tradition.

[2] This is the meaning of Matt. iii.11 where—at any rate according to the evangelist's interpretation ($\pi\hat{\upsilon}\rho$ must be understood in verse 11 as in verses 10 and 12 to be the fire of judgement)—baptism by water is contrasted with the double baptism performed by him who comes. The voice from heaven too (verse 17) apparently assumes the connection of John's baptism with the final baptism of wrath. He who of his own free will placed himself under $\grave{o}\rho\gamma\acute{\eta}$ stands in reality under $\epsilon\grave{\upsilon}\delta o\kappa\acute{\iota}a$ (cf. p. 132).

[3] For the expectation of a river of fire ($\pi o\tau\alpha\mu\grave{o}s$ $\pi\upsilon\rho\acute{o}s$, *diluvium ignis*) at the end cf. also Sib. II.196 ff., 315, 252 f.; Pseudo-Melito 12, in J. C. Th. von Otto, *Corpus Apologetarum Christianorum Saeculi Secundi* IX (1872), p. 432 and on this Eisler, *op. cit.* (p. 111, n. 2), p. 109.

of baptism rests, still remained concealed, namely its association with Jesus' death and redemptive power. Since by his death Jesus took upon himself God's whole wrath against the world (p. 131), the power to deliver from his wrath lies in the baptism's sacrament of death. But whilst John's baptism awards this gift only as a promise, the baptism of Christ awards it in actual fact.

(iii) The third group of images, comprising the symbols of the cup and the bowl, the wine and wine-press of wrath, also stands in a certain family relationship to the two groups of water and of fire.[1] In the NT (cf. p. 31) the image of the cup of wrath[2] and of the wine belonging to it ranks amongst the favourite metaphors of the book of Revelation, and indeed it describes two different (cups and) wines of wrath corresponding to the two main effects of divine wrath (cf. p. 128). The one kind symbolises the punishment of $\beta a\sigma a\nu\iota\sigma\mu\delta s$ (Rev. xiv.10, here as an epexegetical parallel $\beta a\sigma a\nu\iota\sigma\theta\dot{\eta}\sigma\epsilon\tau a\iota$ $\dot{\epsilon}\nu$ $\pi\nu\rho\dot{\iota}$ $\kappa a\dot{\iota}$ $\theta\epsilon\dot{\iota}\omega$, cf. xvi.19). The other is the judgement of wrath on apostasy which proceeds according to the fundamental principle that God's wrath punishes sin by means of sin; thus in Rev. xiv.8; (Babylon) $\dot{\eta}$ $\dot{\epsilon}\kappa$ $\tau o\hat{\nu}$ $o\ddot{\iota}\nu o\nu$ $\tau o\hat{\nu}$ $\theta\nu\mu o\hat{\nu}$ $\tau\hat{\eta}s$ $\pi o\rho\nu\epsilon\dot{\iota}as$ $a\dot{\nu}\tau\hat{\eta}s$ $\pi\epsilon\pi\delta\tau\iota\kappa\epsilon\nu$ $\pi\dot{a}\nu\tau a$ $\tau\dot{a}$ $\ddot{\epsilon}\theta\nu\eta$ *who has made all nations drink the fierce wine[3] of her*

---

[1] The frequent metaphorical phrase *to pour out wrath* (cf. p. 31) can be understood by combining the metaphors adduced in (ii) and (iii); in the NT, cf. especially Rev. xvi.1 ff.

[2] The image occurs also in the recently discovered Qumran manuscripts, 1 Qp Hab XI (on Hab. ii.16); cf. O. Eissfeldt, 'Der gegenwärtige Stand der in Palästina gefundenen Handschriften 2,' Th LZ 74 (1949), col. 96. For the origin of the image, cf. H. Gressmann, *Der Ursprung der isr.-jüdischen Eschatologie* (1905), pp. 129 ff. and P. Volz, *Der Prophet Jeremia* (1928), pp. 392 f.; cf. TWNTV p. 166, n. 26.

[3] The interpretation given here is not unchallenged. Usually $\theta\nu\mu\delta s$ is understood in the sense of *passion*, thus perhaps *the wine of her passionate ungodliness*. But xviii.6 $\dot{\epsilon}\nu$ $\tau\hat{\omega}$ $\pi o\tau\eta\rho\dot{\iota}\omega$ $\dot{\omega}$ $\dot{\epsilon}\kappa\dot{\epsilon}\rho a\sigma\epsilon\nu$

fornication, similarly in xviii.3.[1] It is the wine and cup of staggering of the OT (e.g. Ps. lx.3 [Heb. 5]; lxxv.8 [Heb. 9]; Isa. li.17, 22) which is brought here to its eschatological fulfilment. It is God who really acts when Babylon in its ungodliness takes or gives God's wine of wrath, as it is described in Jer. li.7 with the same imagery: *Babylon was a golden cup in the Lord's hand, making all the earth drunken; the nations drank of her wine, therefore the nations went mad.* This means that God's wrath itself offers the cup of fornication, i.e. of apostasy from God, and punishes all who drink it. Rom. i.18-32 is the commentary on this thesis.[2]

κεράσατε αὐτῇ διπλοῦν makes it probable that the οἶνος τοῦ θυμοῦ in xiv.8 and 10 are similar. It may be said that we have here a certain mixture of metaphors. But it is the same cup of wrath, even though filled with different kinds of wine of wrath. The interpretation that θυμός = *poison* (as, e.g. in Deut. xxxii.33) is quite unlikely, for although in Rev. xiv.8, xviii.3 the wine might be poison, yet it could not be this in xiv.10, xvi.19, xix.15; similarly W. Bousset, *Kommentar z. Apokalypse* ([6]1906), p. 385; E. Lohmeyer, *Kommentar z. Apokalypse* (1926), pp. 121 f.; F. Büchsel in TWNT III, 168; a different view in H. Seesemann, TWNT V, p. 167.

[1] On the other hand in xvii.2 the wine (οἶνος τῆς πορνείας) is only a metaphor for the seductive power of ungodliness which confuses the senses.

[2] Is the cup which Jesus asks his almighty father to take away from him (Mark xiv.36: παρένεγκε τὸ ποτήριον τοῦτο ἀπ' ἐμοῦ) also God's cup of wrath? In that case Jesus would fear that this cup would bring to an end the loving intercourse on which his existence rested. Then the cry from the cross that God had forsaken him (Mark xv.34 and parallels) would be the indication that he had nevertheless been obliged to drink it (so Procksch, cf. p. 132). Now it is true that in the OT such a cup with no further description is occasionally the cup of wrath (e.g. Jer. xlix.12). But apart from the fact that it is hardly possible to distinguish between the cup of anger and that of suffering (TWNT III, p. 168), it is more probable from Jesus' own usage of the image (Mark x.38; John xviii.11) that in Gethsemane he means the cup of death. Cf. also Asc. Isa. v.13.

The different form of the metaphor represented by the seven bowls of wrath[1] (Rev. xvi.1 ff.) agrees with the first conception of the cup of wrath ($=\beta\alpha\sigma\alpha\nu\iota\sigma\mu\acute{o}s$). These bowls, the third of the great apocalyptic groups of seven, are poured out over the earth. The contents of the $\dot{\epsilon}\pi\tau\grave{\alpha}$ $\phi\iota\acute{\alpha}\lambda\alpha\iota$ $\tau o\hat{v}$ $\theta\upsilon\mu o\hat{v}$ $\tau o\hat{v}$ $\theta\epsilon o\hat{v}$ are *the wrath of God who lives for ever and ever* (xv.7); they are actually in the form of the seven last plagues with which the wrath of God is consummated.

The metaphor of the wine-press appears in the book of the Revelation in two passages.[2] In xix.15 it is again the same wine of God's wrath (as in xiv.10, xvi.19) which Christ on his return himself prepares, treading the wine-press. In xiv.19 f. it is the grapes full of men's sins which are pressed out in the $\lambda\eta\nu\grave{o}s$ $\tau o\hat{v}$ $\theta\upsilon\mu o\hat{v}$ $\tau o\hat{v}$ $\theta\epsilon o\hat{v}$ and the wine is their blood which streams from the wine-press and becomes a great lake (verse 20).

(iv) Lastly we must mention once more the phrase $\theta\eta\sigma\alpha\upsilon\rho\acute{\iota}\zeta\epsilon\iota\nu$ $\mathring{o}\rho\gamma\acute{\eta}\nu$ (Rom. ii.5; cf. p. 104) which hints at the paradoxical metaphor of a store of wrath[3] accumulated in heaven. It forms the counterpart to the conception of a completely different 'treasure in heaven' (Matt. xix.21, vi.20; Luke xii.33 f.). Whilst the interest on this store from profit and earnings is already enjoyed in this life according to Jewish ideas and only the capital remains to be handed out at the end, the store of wrath grows until the last day in order to be paid with

[1] Their prototype in the OT is probably the threat of the seven-fold chastisement of wrath in Lev. xxvi.18, 21, 24, 28, or even the six men of Ezek. ix.2.

[2] Their OT prototype is Isa. lxiii.1-6; Joel iii [Heb. iv], 13; cf. G. Bornkamm, TWNT IV, pp. 260-262.

[3] It may also be found in rabbinic writings, e.g. J. Peah, 1, 15d 64: . . . *four things punished in a man in this world, while the store remains in that world—idolatry, adultery, bloodshed, blasphemy*. So also T. Peah, 1, 2 (cf. W. Bauer on Peah 1, 1b; G. Schlichting, *Der Toseftatraktat Pea* (Diss. Tübingen, 1936), *ad loc.*).

compound interest. Hence that day is called ἡμέρα
ὀργῆς (Rom. ii.5).[1]

v. *The objects and the instruments of divine wrath*

(a) *Its objects*

In the NT too God is not provoked to anger arbit-
rarily; wrath is not a trait of the divine nature (cf. p.
26). As in the old historical works and in the prophets
(cf. pp. 26 ff.), the first object of God's anger is the
ancient people of God, the Jews. Already the Baptist's
preaching speaks of this (Matt. iii.7 and parallels): *Do
you think that you can escape from the wrath to come?* Jesus
takes up the idea (Luke xxi.23): ἔσται ἀνάγκη μεγάλη ἐπὶ
τῆς γῆς καὶ ὀργὴ τῷ λαῷ τουτῷ. This means: *the messianic
distress will come upon the whole earth*[2] *and God's wrath will
fall particularly upon this people.* Elsewhere too when
Jesus speaks about anger, he is referring to the Jews (cf.
Mark iii.5; Luke xiv.21; Matt. xxii.7 and probably also
xviii.34), and Paul too sees things at first in the same

[1] Many of the images mentioned have a trait of gruesome irony
of their own: a treasure is really a joyful thing (Matt. vi.21 and
parallels; xiii.44), the harvest (Matt. iii.12) and the vintage in
particular (Rev. xiv.18 ff.) are times of rejoicing (cf. Isa. ix.3
[Heb. 2]); wine really gladdens man's heart (Ps. civ.15) and the
cup is really a typical metaphor for joy and salvation (cf. Ps.
cxvi.13). But all this by its association with ὀργή is now changed
into its opposite. Something similar in the employment of
metaphors may be observed elsewhere too in the Bible.

[2] It is a matter of choice whether γῆ is to be understood simply,
as in verse 25, of the whole earth or simply of 'the land' (TWNT
I, pp. 676, 677), i.e. Palestine as in iv.25 (cf. F. Hauck, *Lukas ad loc.*)
In spite of the parallelism which rather suggests the second
alternative, I consider the first one to be correct, firstly because
verse 25 is so close as to make a different meaning in verse 23
unlikely, and secondly because already at that time 'the land' in
the messianic promises was frequently understood in Judaism in
a general sense to mean the whole earth.

light; cf. especially I Thess. ii.16 (cf. p. 107), also Rom. ii.5—the Jews primarily are the impenitent ones who despise God's μακροθυμία; and in Rom. iv.15—the Jews primarily are the people of the law which for them ὀργὴν κατεργάζεται.

But by no means only the Jews are concerned. In face of God's wrath all mankind are alike. For they are all born with the same nature: they are all bound to the *desires* and *passions of the flesh* and hence they all lie under ὀργή. Hence all men were originally *by nature* τέκνα ὀργῆς (Eph. ii.3),[1] and it is equally true (cf. pp. 108 f.) that the σκεύη ὀργῆς like the σκεύη ἐλέους, derive *not only from the Jews but also from the Gentiles* (Rom. ix.22 ff.). The book of Revelation presents a particularly full picture of the operations of wrath.[2] Here it comes upon all nations (Rev. xi.18, xiv.8, xviii.3, xix.15), and all classes (though particularly the powerful and the rich, Rev. vi.15 ff.), all mankind (Rev. xiv.19, xvi.1), because they became worshippers of Anti-christ (Rev. xiv.9 ff.), and most of all Babylon, the embodiment of the godless, tyrannical, totalitarian power (Rev. xiv.8, xvi.19).

Now Babylon is associated so closely with the 'beast' (e.g. in Rev. xvii.3) that it itself acquires a share in the character of a power of the next world which resists God. This is the special enrichment of the picture in the book of Revelation—God's wrath is also directed against the devil and all powers opposed to God, as had become evident already in the manifestation of God in Christ (p. 92). Indeed the *dies irae* is intended for them in the first place; and in fact here there is presented

---

[1] The ἡμεῖς in this passage means either *we Jewish Christians*—οἱ λοιποί are the Gentile Christians—or *we Christians*, then ὡς καὶ οἱ λοιποί means: *as the rest of mankind* (i.e. are still so today).

[2] In the passages of the book of Revelation listed here, ὀργή occurs only in vi.16 f., xi.18, xiv.10, xvi.19 and xix.15; all the rest have only θυμός which is preferred in this book (p. 120, n. 2).

9

a picture of two powers coming into conflict with each other in wrath. Here the devil is fighting with his θυμὸς μέγας (p. 77)—symbolised in Rev. xii.17 by the image of the furious dragon (καὶ ὠργίσθη ὁ δράκων)— and at his side the nations of Rev. xi.18 raging against God and his kingdom. It is the great eschatological counter-wrath opposing the wrath of God, displayed with colouring from the Psalms, so that the drama of the book of the Revelation can be understood as the conflict between two ὀργαί.

(b) *Its Instruments*

It comes to the point of struggles between the ὀργαί because God himself in his wrath with mankind allows 'the demons to fume and rage'. Hence this means that the powers opposing God become the instruments of the divine wrath against the world.[1] 'The power and rights of Satan and his hosts are derived from the wrath of God.'[2]

The wrath of the devil has reached the position of a servant subordinated to divine wrath by a circuitous route. At the first stage the powers opposing God replace divine wrath independently; not until the second stage is their service made subject to him. The first stage is due to the attempt to remove as far as possible from God the catastrophes which formerly were themselves considered to be indications of divine wrath (pp. 29 f.). The second stage arose out of the concern to close the door against the dualism threatened by the first one. For the first one compare I Chron. xxi.1 with II Sam. xxiv.1 (p. 36); Jub. xlix.4 with Exod. xii.12;

---

[1] An attempt which is scarcely justified has been made to find in Rom. xiii.4, also the idea, in a somewhat different sense, of using the powers of the next world εἰς ὀργήν (cf. p. 102, n. 2).

[2] Althaus *op. cit.* (p. 84, n. 2) II, p. 260.

I Cor. x.10[1] with Num. xiv.34 ff.; Heb. ii.4 with Gen. iii.19b.[2] For the second stage, cf. Ecclus. xxix.28 ff.: *there are winds[3] created for vengeance and in his wrath lay on their scourges heavily; in the time of consummation they pour out their strength and shall appease the wrath of their maker.* The spirits are imagined as God's agents who *in his wrath scourge heavily*; but they will do so because *in the time of consummation*, i.e. evidently in the last days immediately before the final judgement, *they will pour out their strength and appease the wrath of their maker.*[4] Thus here, it seems, is an anticipation of the last judgement as the furious raging of ministering spirits, by which the final paroxysm of divine wrath at the judgement itself will be soothed. A second idea that the devil is assessed and put in his place lies behind the assertions in the NT even where the devil apparently places himself independently beside and in opposition to God. He is never

---

[1] The ὀλεθρευτής is either an angel of destruction (p. 85 ; p. 103, n. 2; cf. p. 64) or again the devil himself (cf. TWNT V, p. 170).

[2] cf. Apoc. Mos. xiv: God's wrath is death (p. 128, n. 1). The divergence in the interpretation of δυνάμενος καὶ ψυχὴν καὶ σῶμα ἀπολέσαι ἐν γεέννῃ in Matt. x.28 (p. 84, n. 1) is due to the conflicting opinions of the Bible itself. The same twofold statements about death are also made about temptation. Conversely God himself takes on the role of accuser in court, which is after all the *opus proprium* of the Satan, i.e. the 'the accuser' κατ᾽ ἐξοχήν (cf. Rev. xii.10); cf. Gen. R. 93 (59b) on Gen. xlv.3 (cf. Wetter, p. 49, n. 1; Str. B. III, p. 220): *How will men one day hold their own before the holy one, . . . who is judge and accuser at the same time?*

[3] It is probably not a question of *winds*—beside the forces of nature enumerated in the following verses—but of *spirits*, i.e. of the personification of these forces described just as if they were persons in verse 31: ἐν τῇ ἐντολῇ αὐτοῦ εὐφρανθήσονται κτλ, i.e. *they rejoice in his commands*, etc.

[4] The transitive use of κοπάζω (*appease*) (mentioned neither by Passow or by Liddell and Scott) seems to be a peculiarity of Ecclus. (cf. in addition xliii.23, xlvi.17 and especially xlviii.10); cf. Helbing, *Kasussyntax*, p. 79.

more than 'God's agent' without knowing or wishing it; he is an instrument of God's wrath, whose function he has only apparently taken over on his own account (cf. I Cor. ii.8).[1]

But at the same time the devil is also the object and victim of divine wrath (pp. 117 f.; also p. 67). Thereby a fundamental law for the divine control of the world is observed, namely that being an instrument of God's wrath involves *eo ipso* being also its victim; a σκεῦος ὀργῆς in the active sense (Jer. 1.25 [LXX, xxvii. 25]) is in itself also a σκεῦος ὀργῆς in the passive sense (Rom. ix.22; p. 108). That was true under the old covenant with regard to the great powers (cf. Isa. x.5-19 with v.25-30 as well as I Chron. xxvii.24 with II Sam. xxiv.1) in relation to Israel. It is true under the new covenant with regard to the Jews in relation to Christ and the new Israel (p. 127), with regard to Judas (cf. Luke xvii.1) and above all with regard to the devil himself, who as the will opposing God is simply the active and passive σκεῦος ὀργῆς of God κατ' ἐξοχήν in relation to the cosmos in this age. At the same time in this matter too the primeval era and the final era are correlated to each other: as the twofold catastrophes at the beginning and at the end of the world's history (p. 111) correspond to each other, so does a judgement of wrath on the devil at the beginning (cf. Vit. Ad. xv f.; Apoc. Mos. xxvi; Jude 6) and another at the end (Rev. xx.10).

Lastly the relationship of the power of the state to the wrath of God must be regarded in this light. The ἐξουσία[2] in Rom. xiii.4 is called: θεοῦ διάκονος εἰς

[1] cf. the excursus on 'Die Täuschung der Geisterwelt durch Christus' (Christ's deception of the spirit world) in H. Lietzmann, *Korintherbriefe* ([3]1931) on I Cor. ii.6.

[2] Although the powers of the next world can play the part of διάκονοι εἰς ὀργήν and of ἔκδικοι in God's service (p. 118), yet to

ὀργὴν¹ ἔκδικος τῷ τὸ κακὸν πράσσοντι. It was considered strange that here the political power appears as the power to execute divine wrath; but it will not do on that account to strike out εἰς ὀργήν which is attested almost

interpret the ἐξουσίαι in Rom. xiii by reference to these powers seems to me very questionable (G. Dehn, 'Engel und Obrigkeit', in *Festschrift für K. Barth* (1936), pp. 90-109; K. Barth, *Rechtfertigung und Recht* (1944), pp. 14-21 (yet in his commentary on Romans, even in the recent edition, K. Barth has not included this interpretation of ἐξουσίαι); O. Cullmann, *Königsherrschaft Christi und Kirche im NT* (1941) pp. 44-48; *Christus und die Zeit* (1946), pp. 169-186 (ET *Christ and Time* (1951), pp. 191-210, where there is on pp. 182 f. (ET pp. 205 f.) a bibliography of this discussion; W. Schweitzer, *Die Herrschaft Christi und der Staat* (1949). In view of phrases like ἕξεις ἔπαινον ἐξ αὐτῆς, τὴν μάχαιραν φορεῖ, φόρους τελεῖτε an unprejudiced reader would always think first of political powers, as Irenaeus already (*Haer.* V.24, 1) perceived correctly. In the NT, especially in the book of the Revelation, it is quite clear that other powers stand behind the politicians, but it cannot be proved, even in spite of I Cor. ii.8, that they are intended to be included in Rom. xiii (cf. G. Kittel, *Christus und Imperator* (1939), pp. 48-54; F. J. Leenhardt, *Le chrétien doit-il servir l'État?* (1939), pp. 36 ff.; E. Brunner, 'Zur christologischen Begründung des Staats', Kirchenblatt für die reformierte Schweiz, 99 (1943), pp. 2-5, 18-23, 34-36; M. Dibelius, *Rom und die Christen im 1. Jahrhundert* (1942), pp. 6 ff.; W. Elert, 'Paulus und Nero', in *Zwischen Gnade und Ungnade* (1948), p. 42, n. 1; H. von Campenhausen, 'Zur Auslegung von Rom xiii; die dämonistische Deutung des ἐξουσία-Begriffes', *Festschrift für A. Bertholet* (1950), pp. 97-113; G. Bornkamm, 'Christus und die Welt in der urchristlichen Botschaft', ZThK 47 (1950), p. 224; TWNT II, p. 562, article on ἐξουσία, which was written, however, before the discussion started by Dehn).

¹ In spite of the usual order of words being better attested, I consider the one just given to be the original one; διάκονος εἰς ὀργήν is parallel with διάκονος εἰς τὸ ἀγαθόν (cf. the same contrast εἰς ἀγαθόν-θυμός II Esdr. viii.22) and it is better to connect ἔκδικος with the dative than with εἰς ὀργήν: *as an agent in matters concerning the working of God's wrath the state administers retribution to the offender*. The order of the words was changed probably because 'God's agent for wrath' seemed to give offence.

unanimously[1] or to find here a reference to the wrath of the authorities.[2] How many heathen people and rulers are mentioned in the Bible as having carried divine wrath into effect (cf. pp. 32 f. with p. 33, n. 2; p. 41). They do so even when they, like the devil, consciously wage war on God and his own; thereby they rage unconsciously actually against themselves as διάκονοι εἰς ὀργὴν ἔκδικοι τῷ τὸ κακὸν πράσσοντι. This is precisely the picture of the power of the state in the book of the Revelation and this explains the inner unity between Rom. xiii and Rev. xiii ff.[3] The ἐξουσίαι can at any time lose their position as agents, thereby they become agents of the devil instead of agents of God, as the imagery of the book of the Revelation shows, and, like their master, they themselves fall all the more into the power of God's wrath, whose instruments they were chosen to be.

(c) The position of the Christians

In face of God's wrath there can be no one who is not affected by it (cf. Rom. iii.23); one can only be exculpated. This is the peculiar position of the 'third race', compared with all the others, with Jews just as much as with Gentiles. Like all the rest it must present itself before God's judgement seat, but through Christ it is delivered from the ὀργή (I Thess. i.10; Rom. v.6) and from κατακρίνεσθαι (I Cor. xi.32; II Thess. i.5 ff.); so

[1] Thus Procksch following the Western Test. It is probably not unwarranted to regard the immediately preceding passage in xii.19 as connected directly with xiii.4 f.: a power of the state has been appointed the agent for the ὀργὴ θεοῦ whom the individual must not on his own account prevent from carrying out his task (cf. O. Cullmann, *Christus und die Zeit* (1940), pp. 177 ff. ET pp. 200 f.).

[2] J. Chr. K. von Hofmann, *Römerbrief* (1868), *ad. loc.* (pp. 536 f.).

[3] This inner unity is thus not only exhibited by the acceptance of the so-called ' "christological foundation" of the state' (against O. Cullmann, *op. cit.* (n. 1) p. 179, ET p. 202).

that looking back with Christ in mind it can confess: we were never meant for wrath; we were prepared from the first (προετοιμάζω in Rom. ix.23) to be σκεύη ἐλέους.

vi. The reasons for and the effects of divine wrath

(a) The reasons for divine wrath

In the NT, as in the OT (p. 39), all motives for divine wrath can be traced back to one fundamental motive, namely man's contempt of God.[1] Paul demonstrates that the whole world, both Jewish and Gentile, stands under the ὀργὴ θεοῦ (Rom. i.18-iii.20). The reason is ἀδικία and ἀσέβεια; the Gentiles' contempt of God is shown by their disregard of the revelation of his nature (δύναμις καὶ θειότης) through what he has created (Rom. i.18, 21 ff.), that of the Jews by their disregard and violation of his will in the law (Rom. ii.17 ff., iii.19 f.). The wrath of Paul in Acts xvii.16 (παρωξύνετο) is like an echo of this divine wrath: its cause is the dishonouring of God by the worship of false gods, like the ζῆλος of Jesus in John ii.15 ff. The NT message clearly shares with that of the OT the explanation of ὀργή as wrath against evil (Rom. xii.19, xiii.4), against παράβασις (iv.15), against ἀδικία (iii.5); cf. especially also Heb. iii.11, iv.3 with the motivation given in iii.10 (ἀεὶ πλανῶνται τῇ καρδίᾳ) and the parallel passages in Eph. v.6 and Col. iii.6, where the ὀργὴ τοῦ θεοῦ, associated perhaps with a kind of traditional catechism,[2] is followed by a list of vices in which the ὀργή of man is also mentioned. The ὀργή of the ἡμέραι ἐκδικήσεως in Luke xxi.22 f. is explicitly linked with the OT and this happens in other passages where the ὀργὴ

---

[1] That this is in fact the common denominator can be gathered especially from Jesus' parables, e.g. Matt. xxii.11 ff., xxv.24 ff., xxi.37 ff.

[2] cf. E. Lohmeyer, Kolosserbrief (⁸1930), ad loc.

ἐρχομένη or μέλλουσα (pp. 98 f.) is mentioned; it must 'come' for the very reason that it has been foretold by the prophets whose picture of the future includes the manifestation of wrath as an integrating feature. But the real reason in both passages is always the fact that men are ἁμαρτωλοί, ἐχθροὶ θεοῦ (Rom. v.8, 10, etc.), that they are apostates. The book of the Revelation carries this explanation of divine wrath further, and into another sphere. Wrath is kindled in Rev. xiv by apostasy from God—not only against the created order as in Rom. i, but also against the power opposing God, the 'beast'. Wrath is discharged not only on indulgence in sin, but on apostasy itself; for πορνεία is actually God's wine of wrath (pp. 113 f.), thus his wrath in action which thereby reaches its highest intensification.

The explanation of the ὀργὴ θεοῦ becomes more profound and stern when it no longer springs from ἁμαρτία against God as contempt of his holy will in the law (or in creation), but as contempt of his holy love in the gospel (Rom. ii.4) (p. 39). However in this case it exhibits a parallel in detail to the contempt of God in the law.[1] The line leading to ὀργή is in the OT: νόμος—παράβασις—ὀργή; in the NT it is: ἐπαγγελία—ἀπιστία—ὀργή. The opposite series is in the former ὑπακοή—τιμή, in the latter πίστις—χάρις—δόξα. Contempt of God's kindness, patience and tolerance (Rom. ii.4) is the decisive reason for ὀργή in the NT. Jesus describes the same thing in the contemptuous refusal of the invitation (Luke xiv.16 ff., especially verse 21) which in the Matthaean variant (xxii.2 ff.) rises to hatred and

---

[1] Both can be called ἀπειθεῖν-ἀπείθεια; in the latter case rather in the sense of disobedience (Eph. v.6, in the former in that of lack of faith, John iii.36). The transition, or rather the mingling of the two, is indicated in Rom. ii.8: ἀπειθεῖν τῇ ἀληθείᾳ, πείθεσθαι τῇ ἀδικίᾳ; cf. also i.18: τὴν ἀλήθειαν ἐν ἀδικίᾳ κατέχειν and the close proximity of ἀπιστία and ἀδικία in Rom. iii.3, 5.

murder. So too does Paul in a corresponding 'anti-semitic' picture of the Jews in I Thess. ii.14 ff.: they said 'no' to Jesus and God replied with 'no' in the form of his ὀργή.

Another reason in the NT for ὀργή is that the response to the love of God is lack of love, to his mercy it is mercilessness, which also increases to hatred and murder (cf. Mark iii.5 f.; Matt. xviii.21 ff.; ἔπνιγεν in verse 28). That too is contempt of God and his χρηστότης. In addition to Mark iii.5 and Matt. xviii.34[1] this is the reason for the ὀργή in Rom. ii.5, in so far as judging is also uncharitable and at the same time an expression of impenitence.[2] This passage makes it clear that the two causes of ὀργή—contempt of God and uncharitableness towards our brother as response to the gospel—are fundamentally one and the same; for the ἀμετανόητος is *eo ipso* merciless. The prototype of both these qualities is the Jews, and especially the Pharisees in the gospel.[3] The NT calls this attitude πρώρωσις τῆς καρδίας (Mark iii.5) or σκληρότης (Rom. ii.5). To this the reply of the ὀργὴ θεοῦ is the 'revenge' (Rom. xii.19) of wounded love in which revenge is at one with his righteousness as a judge.[4]

The line indicated here for the occasion of God's wrath in the NT cuts across a final cause which is hard to understand. Paul seems to know something about the fact that behind all other reasons for ὀργή there stands the really decisive one, the will of God himself.

[1] On the other hand in the parable of the prodigal son, the second part of which is akin to this, only the ὀργή of the uncharitable brother is mentioned (Luke xv.28), and no word is said of an angry reaction, in itself very natural, on the part of the father—in fact just the opposite (cf. verse 31 τέκνον, also Matt. xx.13-15).

[2] cf. Schrenk, pp. 20 f.

[3] cf. J. Schniewind, *Das Gleichnis vom verlorenen Sohn* (1940), pp. 35-38.

[4] cf. P. Althaus (p. 84, n. 2) on Rom. xii.19.

Here the mysterious possibility of a *praedestinatio ad iram*
appears in the background when Paul (Rom. ix.22)
speaks of σκεύη ὀργῆς κατηρτισμένα εἰς ἀπώλειαν which
God 'wills' to use to demonstrate the power of his
wrath; for κατηρτισμένα means, not that *they had de-
veloped, were ready* (for destruction),[1] but that because of
the parallel ἃ προητοίμασεν in verse 23: *they have been
prepared for this by God.* There is evidence for such a
preparation for divine wrath by an indirect statement
in I Thess. v.9: οὐκ ἔθετο ἡμᾶς ὁ θεὸς εἰς ὀργήν, ἀλλὰ
εἰς περιποίησιν σωτηρίας. *God has destined us* (i.e. the
Christians) *to the attainment of salvation;* but us alone; for
the others there is in fact a θέσθαι by God εἰς ὀργήν.
The same thought lies behind Paul's ideas concerning
the law in Rom. iv.15: ὁ γὰρ νόμος ὀργὴν κατεργάζεται,
and for Paul this is not a *parergon* of the law, it is its
opus proprium; it is the purpose of the law to place men
definitely under the wrath, ἵνα πᾶν στόμα φραγῇ καὶ
ὑπόδικος γένηται πᾶς ὁ κόσμος τῷ θεῷ (Rom. iii.19).
Such ideas never occur in isolation, but are always
embedded in statements about ἐκδίκησις and similar
subjects. This means that in such cases always, before
all else, the guilt of man must be perceived. Here
human guilt and God's will form a network just as
inextricable as elsewhere the temptation of the devil
on the one hand and human original sin, with ever
fresh actual lapses, on the other (Eph. ii.2 f.).

(b) The causes and effects of divine wrath are inseparable

We enter into the final impenetrable darkness of
divine wrath when we recognise that the effects which
it produces itself are its most important causes, and that
again all great acts of divine wrath become an equal
number of reasons for fresh discharges of wrath. What

---

[1] Thus von Hofmann, *op. cit.* (p. 122, n. 2), p. 401.

the Jews did and that for which they are blamed so severely, had to happen in accordance with God's own plan. Even they, with their hatred of God venting its furious rage on Jesus, were the instruments of this purpose of love and salvation, and yet on that account God's wrath fell upon them. The very thing which caused the anger is imposed on them as a retributory punishment, namely complete rejection of Christ.[1] Thus we find ourselves here in a sequence which appears to human logic as a *circulus vitiosus* of guilt and punishment, and this belongs to the most terrible discoveries in the Bible. Sin and unbelief, the two main causes of the ὀργὴ θεοῦ are at the same time its effects. Paul demonstrates this in Rom. i; it is probably also the meaning of Rom. ix.22: God reveals his wrath in the hardening of the σκεύη ὀργῆς (e.g. the Pharaoh) whom he has long tolerated. This applies also to the Jews.[2] Here it is impossible to distinguish what is sin and what is destiny. Divine wrath acts on the divine principle[3] which requites like with like, which lets the deed recoil on the head of the perpetrator.[4]

---

[1] cf. Filson, p. 43.

[2] 'The reality of the hardening shows up the power of God's wrath which holds sway over man also in his sin (Althaus, *op. cit.* (p. 84, n. 2) on Rom. ix.17 f.). Without the use of the word 'wrath' the unity of guilt and the fall, as a thing prepared by God, is expressed with excellent brevity in I Peter ii.8: προσκόπτουσιν τῷ λόγῳ ἀπειθοῦντες, εἰς ὃ καὶ ἐτέθεσαν, thereby giving what is fundamentally a description of the effects of his wrath on the unbelievers (cf. G. Stählin, *Skandalon* (1930), pp. 197 f.).

[3] Without any possibility of being itself this principle, against Wetter, p. 20.

[4] cf. also Matt. xxvi.52b; xxvii.25. Jewry too recognised something of this, although not in the full depth of the NT discovery; cf. Ab. 4, 2: *the performance of one duty involves the performance of another, and one transgression involves another; since the reward of performing one duty is to perform another, and the reward of a transgression is to transgress again.*

(c)　The effects of divine wrath

In what we have just said the most profound reply of
the NT to the question concerning the effects of divine
wrath has been anticipated. In this reply the non-
biblical and the OT world had approached each other
in a striking manner (pp. 7 ff., 33 f.), in so far as in all
these cases natural catastrophes and those in the
nation's life are traced back to God's wrath. The OT
(e.g. in Ps. xc.7-11) exposes with particular emphasis
the fundamental connection between God's wrath and
death[1] and the NT follows in its footsteps;[2] cf. in particular Rom. i.18 ff. (verse 32 ἄξιοι θανάτου) and Rom.
xiii.1 ff. (μάχαιρα—ὀργή).

Furthermore, in the picture of eschatological wrath
the correspondence of ὀργή and θάνατος is replaced by
that of ὀργή and ἀπώλεια (cf. Rom. ix.22; Rev. xiv ff.),
the prelude to which is the destruction of Jerusalem as a
phenomenon of ὀργή (Luke xxi.23 and an exact parallel
in the parable in Matt. xxii.7). But in fact the
most terrible form of the eschatological ἀπώλεια is
not annihilation, not being snuffed out, but eternal
βασανισμός[3] (Rev. xiv.10 f.; xx.10 et passim; also Matt.
xviii.34): the judgement of wrath is just as 'boundless'
as previously compassion had been (cf. verse 27, 24).

But the most real and characteristic effect of ὀργή in
the NT is unbelief, apostasy and what follows from it,
just as the NT considers μὴ πιστεύοντες and ἀπολλύμενοι
to be equivalent. Thus the very thing generally

---

[1] According to one of the Pseudepigrapha even God's wrath and
the universal fate of death are identical, namely when ὀργή is
considered to be the *punishment of wrath*. In Apoc. Mos. xiv Adam
says to Eve: *What have you wrought in us, and brought upon us great
wrath which is death lording it over all our race?*

[2] cf. amongst others Bartholomäi, p. 258.

[3] cf. Wisdom xi.9: *they learned how the ungodly were tormented,
being judged with wrath.*

supposed to be the cause of ὀργή becomes its effect. It is this which in Rom. i leads far beyond the OT pronouncements, even though these Pauline thoughts may be called a more penetrating modification of the Deuteronomic pattern of retribution (p. 33). The chaos of ancient immorality, and indeed of all human immorality, is a dispensation of the ὀργὴ θεοῦ according to the revelation bestowed upon faith. That is even indicated formally by the ingenious construction of this section: the threefold (μετ)ήλλαξαν (verses 23, 25, 26) correspond to the threefold παρέδωκεν. Here cause and effect are one and the same; the pattern which consists in linking cause and effect as modern man's view of the world, is shattered by the force of divine wrath.

vii. *Deliverance from the wrath of God*

(*a*) The NT shares with the non-biblical[1] and the OT world[2] the desire to escape from divine wrath, or to avert it altogether.

(*b*) Since in the NT the prospect of the wrath to come dominates the picture, the question how to be delivered from it is asked and answered also at the very beginning, in the preaching of the Baptist. The reply is given in these words: μετανοεῖτε . . . ποιήσατε οὖν καρπὸν ἄξιον τῆς μετανοίας in Matt. iii.2, 8, and the promise of deliverance is baptism, in so far as it anticipates the judgement of wrath as a symbol which is more than a symbol, and by means of the anticipation ensures that the judgement itself will be averted (pp. 111 f.).[3] But this

---

[1] cf. pp. 6 ff.; cf. F. Heiler, *Das Gebet* ([5]1921), pp. 87-89; ET *Prayer* (1932), pp. 33-35 *et passim*.

[2] cf. pp. 42 ff.; also Cr. Kö, pp. 811 f.

[3] The same train of thought—baptism to allay the wrath—is the background already in the legend in Vit. Ad. vi-xi: Adam and Eve undertake in the Jordan, or it may be in the Tigris, their own baptism, which is intended to procure their deliverance from

deliverance is not obtained *ex opere operato*. That seems
to be the error of the Pharisees, and the Baptist pro-
ceeded against this first heresy concerning baptism with
the utmost severity: γεννήματα ἐχιδνῶν, τίς ὑπέδειξεν ὑμῖν
φυγεῖν ἀπὸ τῆς μελλούσης ὀργῆς; in Matt. iii.7. As *vipers'
brood*, which means *children of the devil*; cf. TWNT V,
pp. 566 ff., they are τέκνα ὀργῆς, destined to the eternal
fire (Matt. xxv.41). *Who warned you*—if anyone, it can
only be the devil—to let yourselves be baptised deceit-
fully, that means: to pretend to repent and thereby to
obtain protection from the judgement of wrath by
deceit.[1] It is not the *opus operatum* of baptism which
saves—everything depends on genuine μετάνοια, which
accepts God's verdict by taking upon itself the judgement of wrath in the symbol of baptism, and which
proves its genuineness precisely by the καρπός it bears
(verses 8-12). This is the only permissible and the only
hopeful way of escape from wrath and even the Pharisees are not excluded from it (verse 8).[2]

divine wrath. The alternative, either to allay the wrath by means
of baptism or to be judged instead by means of fire—is put forward
in Sib. IV.165, 189, 178. Here the 'baptism' in the river is
combined with loud appeals for forgiveness (cf. I Peter iii.21),
whilst Adam and Eve (in Vit. Ad.) pray for deliverance silently.

[1] Akin to this is the refusal of a sacrifice from the ungodly for
the purpose of appeasing the *ira deorum* in Cicero, *De Legibus* II,
22; cf. p. 9.

cf. T. Zahn, *Kommentar z. Matthäusev.* (²1905), pp. 138 f.;
A. Schlatter, *Matt.* 69 ff. On the other hand Jesus relies on the
possibility for his own to escape from the doom of wrath during
the messianic woes, literally by flight (Luke xxi.21). The sentence
'no deliverance by baptism without repentance' in the sense of the
Baptist, as later in that of Jesus and the apostles, carries the same
weight as the other, 'no salvation by repentance without baptism'.
It may be said that already John's baptism (like the Passover) is a
genuine pre-Christian sacrament, in which salvation is effected
by means of its being bound up with God's command and its
physical performance just as much as with the affirmation of the
recipient.

(c) The apostolic *kerygma* links the deliverance from God's wrath with Jesus. Jesus is he who delivers even now (I Thess. i.10). It is Jesus who some day will deliver from the future wrath (Rom. v.9). Only through him are we certain that we are not destined to wrath (I Thess. v.9 f.). Through him we are even now σωζόμενοι just as he is even now the ῥυόμενος. The deliverance is present and future at the same time, corresponding to the twofold temporal nature of eschatology. Why is deliverance from wrath associated with Jesus? Because we are justified by his blood, because we are reconciled by his death (Rom. v.9 f.), that is to say, there is no longer any condemnation for us (viii.1), we are no longer enemies (v.10). Or may we say: because Jesus has tasted God's wrath for us? Attempts have been made to base the affirmative answer to this question[1] on the scene at Gethsemane and the words from the cross in Matthew and Mark. R. Otto[2] would regard the struggle in Gethsemane in the light of the numinous with its *mysterium* and its *tremendum* and show that the nearest comparison to this conception of it is Jacob's struggle at the Jabbok and the attack on Moses at the lodging place (p. 36). He says it was principally

---

[1] An affirmative answer to this question is given, e.g. by J. T. Beck, 'Der Zorn Gottes', in *Chr. Reden* V (²1871), p. 200; H. J. Holtzmann, *Lehrbuch der neutestamentlichen Theologie* II, (²1911), p. 122: The wrath beneath which the dying (Jesus) seems to be placed has been effectively spent at his death. Similarly Procksch: divine wrath is broken by the sacrificial death of Christ. Also K. Barth, *Kirchliche Dogmatik* II, 1 (²1946), p. 444, ET *Church Dogmatics* (1957), speaks of 'his enduring the eternal wrath of God'. A negative reply is given by Ritschl, *Rechtfertigung und Versöhnung* II, pp. 155 f.; cf. also W. Hasenzahl, *Die Gottesverlassenheit des Christus* (1938), pp. 138-148, where admittedly the question of ὀργή is hardly touched upon, and also Althaus, *op. cit.* (p. 84, n. 2), II, pp. 259-261.

[2] *Das Heilige* (²⁶⁻²⁸1947), p. 106; ET *The Idea of the Holy* (1928), p. 88.

a grappling with divine wrath, and the victory over it already means that the decision has been reached. Similarly Procksch considers that the cup for the removal of which Jesus prays (Mark xiv.36) is the cup of wrath (p. 112, n. 2); Jesus shudders at the final depths of being forsaken by God according to the impressive representation in Luke xxii.44. The angel who in the gospel appears only at crucial points in the events personifies the nearness of God in the threatened abandonment by him (verse 43).[1] But Jesus is not spared the extremity of suffering; his prayer was not answered.[2] This is expressed in a deeply moving way by his last cry in Matthew and Mark: *Eli, eli, lama sabachthani?* For to be abandoned by God means to stand under wrath. That is the prevailing view of the OT: he who provokes God to anger is abandoned by him, and vice versa (Deut. xxxi.17, xxxii.19 f.; Isa. liv.8; Ps. xxvii.9, lxxxix.47).

It must of course be admitted that Jesus' passion is never connected directly with God's wrath; at any rate it is never said *expressis verbis* that Jesus stood under wrath.[3] On the contrary it is stated expressly (Luke ii.40, 52; Mark i.11; Matt. xii.18, xvii.5), that εὐδοκία and χάρις rest on Jesus from beginning to end. It is true that the voice from heaven at the baptism can be understood as a sign that Jesus when he accepted baptism, the symbol of the judgement of wrath, submitted himself to it (p. 112, n. 2). That was the πρέπον which the Baptist could not understand, and so the voice said to this Jesus, who though innocent took God's wrath upon

[1] cf. E. Schick, *Die Botschaft der Engel* (³1949), pp. 128-130.

[2] Hebrews v.7: οὐκ εἰσακουσθείς (according to Harnack's conjecture). Gal. iii.13 also says something similar.

[3] Nevertheless perhaps Jesus himself gives a hint in his allegory of the fire in Luke xxiii.31: Even Jesus, although he is 'green wood', will be thrown (i.e. by God) into the fire, i.e. the judgement of wrath (p. 110).

himself, 'not ὀργή but εὐδοκία'. That which was pro-
mised to Jesus when he anticipates taking our place on
the cross, is denied him on the cross itself, in order that
just because he bears it, he may take away God's wrath
from us (cf. Rom. v.9 as well as the parallel αἴρειν
ἁμαρτίαν in John i.29).

At any rate it certainly belongs inextricably to the
message of the NT that by Jesus' death deliverance
from the wrath to come is guaranteed and therefore
freedom from the present wrath is granted as well, and
this is decisive; for wrath is the real power which
destroys.[1] In Christ alone a breach is made in eternal
wrath. In him alone can we view as one whole the
scandalising tension between God's wrath and his love.[2]

If deliverance from eternal wrath is granted in
Christ alone,[3] then everything depends on whether a

[1] Althaus, *op. cit.* (p. 84, n. 2) II, p. 260 in a comment upon
Greek theologians and K. Heim. However it seems to me that
the view of the NT taken as a whole attaches equal weight to the
two propositions: 'Christ is the saviour from divine wrath and
condemnation' and 'Christ is the great divine counter-action
against Satan's rebellion', cf. Stauffer, *Theologie* (²1947), p. 4
(ET, p. 19) and frequently, especially pp. 127-130. (ET, pp. 146 ff.).

[2] cf. Althaus, *op. cit.* (p. 84, n. 2) II, p. 32; R. Bultmann,
Theologie des NT (1948), p. 283, ET *Theology of the NT* I (1952),
p. 288.

[3] There are no analogies in the ancient world to the Christ who
as judge is the representative of wrath and yet at the same time is
the only deliverer from it. Three passages come relatively
nearest to the thought of the NT, although in a different way:
(1) Livy 8, 9, 10 (p. 11), where admittedly the thought that the
deity itself sends the propitiatory sacrifice to appease the wrath, is
only a beautiful idea (*sicut caelo missus*); but the willingness of
Decius to offer himself voluntarily as a sacrifice is a proper
analogy. (2) The offer of Moses to expose himself in place of the
people to divine wrath (Exod. xxxii.32) and (3) the rendering in
the Midrash of Ps. vii.6 [Heb. 7] (p. 85, n. 2) in which God
himself is summoned to fight against his wrath. Cf. in addition also
the interpretation of Num. xxi in Wisdom xvi.5 ff.

man rejects Christ or appropriates what Christ is and brings—or more correctly, whether he lets himself be appropriated. He who rejects him remains under wrath; he who accepts him is free. *Either he must dread the wrath to come or love the present mercy—one of the two* (Ign. Eph. xi.1). Freedom from God's wrath is bound up with faith in Christ (John iii.36). By faith in him we possess the eschatological gift of freedom from wrath as a present reality. By the baptism with water as a preliminary judgement we acknowledge the right of the real baptism of judgement, that of fire; and thus this ἀντίτυπον of the overflowing wrath delivers us from this wrath itself.[1] But the power of the ἀντίτυπον rests on the fact that through it the baptised person has a share with Christ who himself bore and destroyed the wrath. By means of the power of Christ given in baptism we become σκεύη ἐλέους instead of σκεύη ὀργῆς, living persons instead of νεκροί; this interpretation of baptism thus approaches very closely that of Rom. vi. The two interpretations do not exclude each other, they are complementary.

Nevertheless the deliverance from wrath obtained through sheer grace is not a possession which cannot be lost. Even after complete forgiveness, even after admission into the fellowship of God's kingdom, a complete rejection is still possible (cf. Matt. xviii.34, xxii. 13), and then those who are rejected fall a prey to the eternal operations of wrath (p. 106), *where the worm never dies and the fire is not quenched.* This too belongs to the *kerygma* of the NT (cf. Rom. ii.16)[2]; yet its final testimony is not to wrath's sea of fire, but to the fountain of compassion in Christ.

[1] cf. A. Schlatter, *Kommentar z. Matthäusev.* (1929), p. 71.

[2] But cf. now W. Michaelis, *Versöhnung des Alls* (1950), especially pp. 55 f.

INDEX OF REFERENCES

GENERAL INDEX